# EUROPEAN IN INDIA

# EUROPEAN IN INDIA

*FROM A COLLECTION OF DRAWINGS*

**CHARLES DOYLEY**

GYAN

*Published by*

Gyan Publishing House
5, Ansari Road
Daryaganj, New Delhi-110002
Phone: 011-47034999, 9811692060
E-mail: books@gyanbooks.com

*Distribution Network*
gyanbooks.com
India, USA, Canada, UK, Australia



ISBN: 978-93-7097-293-3 (PB)
First Published, 1813

2nd Impression 2025

*Printed at:* Gyan Press, Delhi.



**EUROPEAN IN INDIA**
Author Charles Doyley

THE

# *EUROPEAN IN INDIA;*

ACCOMPANIED WITH

A BRIEF HISTORY OF

Ancient and

**MODERN INDIA,**

*&c. &c. &c.*

THE

# EUROPEAN IN INDIA;

*FROM A COLLECTION OF DRAWINGS,*

BY

CHARLES DOYLEY, ESQ.

ENGRAVED BY J. H. CLARK AND C. DUBOURG:

WITH A PREFACE AND COPIOUS DESCRIPTIONS,

BY CAPTAIN THOMAS WILLIAMSON;

ACCOMPANIED WITH

## A Brief History of

## ANCIENT AND MODERN INDIA,

FROM THE EARLIEST PERIODS OF ANTIQUITY TO THE TERMINATION OF THE LATE MAHRATTA WAR,

BY F. W. BLAGDON, ESQ.

LONDON:

PUBLISHED AND SOLD BY EDWARD ORME, BOND STREET, CORNER OF BROOK STREET, PRINTSELLER AND PUBLISHER TO HIS MAJESTY AND HIS ROYAL HIGHNESS THE PRINCE REGENT.

PRINTED BY J. F. DOVE, 22, ST. JOHN'S SQUARE, CLERKENWELL.

1813.

# LIST OF PLATES.

# PREFACE.

THE numerous and highly respectable class of readers who thirst for knowledge; and the many whose friends and relatives may have visited India, or may now be resident there, will not, I flatter myself, find this Work unworthy their attention: to them it will, I hope, at least, prove entertaining; while its value may be much enhanced with a large portion of those who may be about to proceed to the East.

The desire to become useful, as well as amusing, has occasioned me to throw much general information into this Preface, which could not with strict propriety have been brought under any particular head, without deviating from the intended limits of the publication: nor could such have been effected without many repetitions, which, though they might swell the volume greatly, would by no means have added either to the information or pleasure of the reader.

Under such circumstances, I hope for approval in the mode I have adopted of compacting such matter, as could not be with propriety allotted to individual descriptions, in this form. An attentive perusal of this Preface will prepare the reader to a competent extent for the consideration of what is detailed in the several Chapters, and enable him to form an accurate judgment of whatever may, either in this, or in any other Work, be offered, as elucidatory of Indian Customs and Manners.

Further, it is to be hoped, many prejudices, formed against the supposed effeminacy of our countrymen in India, may be at least softened, if not altogether removed. We are too apt to judge of what may be practised in other climates by what we are able to do, or to bear, in our own: this greatly resembles the man, who, being half frozen, wishes to change his situation for the sufferings induced by extreme heat; judging, from his immediate feelings, that no excess of the latter power could overcome him, or even cause him to complain! The experience of many has, however, proved the fallaciousness of such a supposition, and affords ample testimony of the necessity of visiting a country, before we censure or condemn the practices of its inhabitants. Perhaps an individual or two, bent on the refutation of the most reasonable assertions, and influenced by a ridiculous determination to support some equally ridiculous hypothesis, may, after suffering extreme inconvenience, and exposing themselves to much danger, have been borne by the vigour of youth through the hazardous enterprize: but the great number of instances that might be adduced of persons so disposed, either giving up the point, or meeting an untimely fate, sufficiently warrants our condemnation of the plan.

The following fact supersedes much argument, and applies most forcibly to the position advanced. A gentleman, who, about seven years ago, proceeded to Bengal in a very high station; and who had been in the habit of consulting his physician very often, thought it necessary, ere he ventured on board ship, to collect the opinions of all his medical friends, as to the plan he must follow in respect to diet, &c. on arriving in India.

Accordingly he was furnished with a multitude of recipes, rules for regimen, and all that could be thought of on the occasion. When the gentleman arrived in India, he submitted the whole to a very clever physician, and asked his opinion regarding their merits. Judge what must have been the gentleman's surprise, on hearing from the doctor, that nine in ten of the prescriptions would infallibly have sent him to "kingdom come!" At length the gentleman produced a short note from a friend, who, in short terms, advised him strongly "to do as he should find the old inhabitants do, and to burn all the instructions he had, at much expense, obtained from the faculty in England." This homely piece of good sense was approved by the doctor; and, being followed, the gentleman not only banished his fears in regard to the climate, but is now returning to Europe in far better health than he could boast of when he left it.

Were any thing wanting to corroborate the above reasonable suggestion, I should lay no small stress on the great age to which numbers of the European inhabitants have lived in Bengal. Many have not been blessed with strong constitutions; but they have, by prudence and forbearance, obviated the greatest dangers; and, as it were, formed an artificial stamina, which has stood them in better stead, than the robust, iron habits of the less temperate. With several the climate has proved highly restorative; but such effect can only be applied to persons labouring under consumptive attacks.

In fact, a young person of good health, disposed to moderation in general, and avoiding the sun during the great heats, may expect to live as long in Calcutta as in any part of the world. On the other hand, it is found, that such as do not touch wine, especially as they advance in years, are not only more subject to disease, but go off more suddenly than those who take a few glasses at their meals. Claret is in general use, as is also Madeira; of which, though it be excellent, much should not be drank; it being apt to heat the blood, and induce fever. Port wine is equally, or more objectionable: though, perhaps, in cases of debility, and especially in a convalescent state after dysentery, its virtues cannot be too much extolled. Spirits, in any form, are baneful. In a warm climate persons are subject to great drought, and one glass follows the other but too rapidly. Various complaints very soon announce themselves, when the inconsiderate tippler speedily passes through the various stages of disease, avoided by society, and his demise is scarcely noticed but by those who may be benefitted by the vacancy.

Landing from the ship in good health is most assuredly an important object; and an early attention to the advice of those, who, from established residence, are competent to guide new-comers along the path of safety, rarely fails of producing the best effects. A fever is, however, to be expected within the first season, the severity of which usually depends on the state of the constitution. This fever, which is considered as a seasoner, either carries off, or endangers the life of all such, as, confiding in the strength of their constitutions, disregard the admonitions of their friends, and expose themselves to the sun, or associate in the midnight revel! Formerly this imprudent class was always receiving recruits; but the havock they sustained rendered the system rather suspicious, and proved a warning to others not to contemn the dictates of experience.

The friends of young men, who are sent to the East Indies, generally fit them out with a great variety of apparel, and other articles, enumerated in the catalogue of the slop-merchant, under the head of " *Necessa-*

*ries.*" Of these, however, a large portion is entirely useless; while, on the other hand, such as would prove serviceable in India, are supplied but scantily. The fact is, that, for ship use, the stock ought to be as much compressed as possible, both in size and number; and the saving in money should be applied towards the purchase of a great variety of indispensable articles, which must be procured on landing. As to taverns, and what we called punch-houses, they are of the worst class; no gentleman can be seen in such of them as receive strangers from Europe. They are the ruin of nine in ten of such as, from the want of a friend on the spot, unhappily o'erstep their thresholds!

A small quantity of furniture, of all kinds, must be provided by every one who is not so lucky as to repair to India under the auspices of some relation or friend. Houses are let in all parts of the country, but with bare walls; as to lodgings, they are unknown. Hospitality has not yet sunk into disrepute; but its practitioners are neither so numerous nor so unreserved as formerly: and though a stranger may sometimes find his European complexion a passport among his countrymen, yet in these days some introduction is looked for, and he is expected to bear his own expenses on all occasions.

There is a tribe of scoundrels, who infest all the avenues communicating with new arrivals, for the most part composed of the lowest order of *Sircars*, or *Kedmutgars*, all of whom speak English, and endeavour to attach themselves to the young men as they arrive; nay, many, at the season of importation, or on hearing that a Company's ship is in the Roads, proceed fifty or sixty miles down the river, with the intent of obtaining employ. All these are the scum of their respective professions, and generally avail themselves of the earliest opportunity to rob, and abscond from their unsuspecting employers; who, happy in finding the means of explaining their wants, and of obtaining information among these artful linguists, lay themselves open to a thousand deceptions, and suffer under the grossest impositions. The *Sircars* may with propriety competite with the most knowing among our Jews, and the *Kedmutgars* in question, commonly termed *Ramjonnies*, from their often assuming that name, would scorn to yield the palm even to the celebrated Ambrose de Lamela! The reader may easily conjecture to what dilemmas an European is often subjected among such worthy attendants; each of whom can speak two languages, and possesses both the will and the means of deception!

Such gentlemen as repair to India, with appointments in the Company's civil or military services, are speedily snatched from this very cruel state of depredation. Their appointments must be made known on arrival, and the persons at the head of offices must consequently be visited; these, much to their credit, never fail to afford every information and assistance, so as to enable the young traveller to be housed in comfort, and in some security. Such as may have friends in the country are set forward to their abodes; and where those are wanting, the greatest attention is paid to supply the deficiency. The latter case is, however, extremely rare; few obtain such very respectable appointments without the additional benefit of an excellent introduction among those of the Establishment to which they are nominated. The greatest sufferers are among the persons attached to the shipping, who generally have no connexions in India, and whose means are very ill-proportioned to their misfortunes.

A large stock of wearing apparel is among the indispensables. Thirty suits will not be found too many. The whole is, generally speaking, of white cotton, manufactured into various cloths; such as dimity, calico for upper and under shirts, upper and under waistcoats, pantaloons, if not made of nankeen, and various other parts of dress. Coats are only used on visits of ceremony, or during the cold season: indeed, though one may be worn on entering the house, the visitor is commonly desired by the host to rid himself of the incumbrance; for which purpose, an upper waistcoat, with sleeves, is always carried in the palankeen. This custom appears singular to persons newly arrived; but its obvious convenience causes its speedy adoption. Some very starched gentlemen have declined it; and, obstinately persisting for many years in the sudorific retention of their heavy woollen dresses, have at length melted into acquiescence.

The climate is certainly by no means favourable to strangers; but, as already remarked, by due precaution, health may usually be insured. Early rising is perhaps more expedient in India than with us; and a hard horse-hair mattress, with European sheeting, should invariably be used. Featherbeds and pillows are unknown; nor could they possibly be admitted, unless under such singular circumstances as have not, I believe, ever been seen in India. In general, outer curtains are useless during more than half the year; but inner curtains, of a fine texture, called *kobbradool*, cannot be dispensed with: these serve to keep out musquitos, which else would devour a new-comer! The bites of these little torments are very acute; and, if scratched, are apt to become extensive ulcers, from which often serious consequences follow.

The floors are never boarded, nor are ceilings in use. The upper timbers are open to the eye; and though, perhaps, not pleasing in the first instance, soon become familiar: to these the large frame *perukahs* are usually slung, as described in the course of this Work. Throughout India, terrace-work is substituted for plank; and, being covered with a fine kind of matting, made of very hard reeds about the thickness of a crow-quill, worked in stripes of perhaps a foot or more in breadth each, as described in several of the Plates, gives a very remarkable neatness to the apartments; many of which, however, are laid with *satringes*, or striped carpets, made of wool, or cotton, during the cold season. Carpets, in imitation of those manufactured at Wilton and Brussells, are now made in India; some of which are of incomparable excellence and beauty.

The walls are invariably plastered with lime, laid very smooth, and finished with a trowel, so that the white cannot rub off. Some rooms are washed with soothing colours to take off the glaze; which, during four or five months, is extremely distressing to the eyes: being done in pannels, they have generally a pleasing effect. The windows are now all glazed, with glass sent from Europe; and such as face the sun are further provided with strong outside Venetians, which serve as shutters.

The necessity which exists for keeping the doors and many windows open, at all times, renders it expedient to guard the candles, which are invariably of wax, from the gusts of wind that would, but for that precaution, speedily blow out every light. Shades, made of glass, are put over such candles as stand on tables; and sconce branches are furnished with similar protections, made in the form of a deep narrow vase: some of these are pourtrayed, as affixed to the walls, in several of the Plates in this Work.

Those who take exercise on horseback are usually up as soon as the day begins to dawn, and return before the sun is well up. In the cold months the ride may be extended; or when the weather proves favourable, the excursion may be delayed till after breakfast; the hour for which is as various as with us in England. Tea, coffee, eggs, toast, and fish, (either fresh or slightly powdered with salt, rice, &c.) form the oriental *dejeuné.* Many gentlemen, especially those from North Britain, add sweetmeats and *soogèe;* the latter corresponding with porridge, or burgoo, only that it is made of wheat-grits instead of being prepared from oats, which are not cultivated in India, though the black species has been frequently found growing wild.

The forenoon is dedicated to business, or to reading, writing, &c.; and, among the idle, the hookah, or eventually, cards, fill the vacuum. Those who have to attend their offices repair to them in their palankeens; and, when their duties are performed, which generally occupy four or five hours, return to their homes, or visit some friend; and, after partaking of a tiffing, undress, and sleep till near sun-set; when they again put on clean clothes of every description, and repair to dinner, which, by that time, is generally ready.

Coffee and tea are served about eight or nine o'clock. Suppers are not usual, except among families in Calcutta, and some out-stations of civil servants. Among the military, early hours are much attended to: and it is rare in cantonments to find any one out of bed at ten o'clock at night, or in bed after five in the morning. Their profession, no doubt, is the principal cause of this regularity; which is, however, greatly increased by the want of female society, there being very few European ladies in India. I should, probably, far exceed their numbers, were I to estimate all, living under the Bengal government, at three hundred!

The truth, is, that matrimony is very expensive, and interferes too much with the duties of a profession, whose members constitute at least two-thirds of the British population in that quarter. Added to this, in the early part of their career, young men attach themselves to the women of the country; and acquire a liking, or taste, for their society and customs, which soon supersedes every other attraction: and as these sable partners (many of whom are, however, of a good colour) accompany the camps; and are, in a measure, inseparable from their keepers, to whom some present a numerous progeny, it is not to be wondered at, that a connexion, commenced in a casual manner, should become firm and lasting. This subject, however amply it might be stated, is of too delicate a nature for me to enlarge upon: it may be expedient, however, to state, that many are under a great mistake, who conclude these connexions to be made by choice, to the neglect of our fair countrywomen: they are the result of necessity.

The great retinue of servants, employed by gentlemen in India, has often been the topic of much inconsiderate censure. The prejudices of the natives are numerous and irreconcileable: they have customs and privileges, established from the earliest days, which, though they may imperceptibly surrender, by long intercourse with Europeans, would produce most serious consequences, if invaded intentionally. These form barriers to many improvements; while, on many occasions, by being protected, they give much support to our Government; to which the natives, both Hindoos and Mahometans, ever look up for a toleration of their respective religion, and for its safety from the usurpations of those of the opposing faith.

With regard to the value of money, we must by no means compute according to our ideas; for, however cheap provisions may be, we find that, in every other respect, the expenses of an individual, in India, are far beyond what would be necessary in Europe. House-rent is dear beyond all imagination; indeed, it must be a very small, mean house, that does not, at Calcutta, let for two hundred rupees monthly; which is equal to three hundred pounds yearly! By this scale many other disbursements must be calculated.

In the course of this Work, the different offices of the various attendants and menials will be described, and their wages, &c. fully detailed. Some of them, indisputably, are attached to absolute luxuries; but, it may be fairly averred, that, in proportion to the rank, income, and consequence, of the average of the gentlemen in India, they possess fewer enjoyments, and exhibit less inclination to excess and dissipation, than persons of corresponding circumstances in Great Britain and Ireland. But, were it otherwise, in lieu of censuring them for indulging in what might appear imprudent, we should probably have a better claim to criticise on the merits of the case, were we to sum up all the dangers, privations, and sufferings, they undergo. A fair examination of the whole subject, would teach us to admire their general character; and to view them, individually, as being by no means unworthy of imitation. With regard to education, morality, and liberal principles, the gentlemen of the Honourable East India Company's Civil and Military Establishments are second to none!!!

THE AUTHOR.

I.

London, Published and Sold by Edw^d Orme March 1st 1813.

# PLATE I.

## AN EUROPEAN GENTLEMAN WITH HIS MOONSHEE, OR NATIVE PROFESSOR OF LANGUAGES.

As a knowledge of the languages of the East is certainly a primary object with such gentlemen as resort to India in the East India Company's service, or with the intention to reside there, for the purpose of trading, &c. a description of the Moonshee, or Linguist, may, with propriety, precede the other more menial occupations.

This profession is not invariably filled by the Mussulmans, though there are very few instances of Hindoos being Moonshees. Nor is it an hereditary occupation, or confined to any particular sect, or tribe, among the former. Moonshees, in general, take great care that their sons become capable of teaching: but there are numerous competitors for this distinguished employ among those whose parents have the means of educating them in a suitable manner. This, indeed, requires but little expense, and but a mere trifle of assiduity. The learning of the generality of Moonshees is extremely confined. Writing a fair hand, an acquaintance with the provincial anomalies, and a readiness at reading the multiplicity of manuscripts which are consigned to them for explanation, and which are sometimes as difficult to decipher as many of our nearly-illegible English writings; added to a copious string of quotations from the Koran, and a general acquaintance with the very few books extant in India, in the Persian language, mostly the lives of great men, or the Poems of Hafiz, &c. may be said to comprise the requisites for being classed among the sages of the East! As to science, it is not only neglected, but despised.

The Moonshee attends daily from breakfast to dinner time; and, eventually, during the evening also. His wages vary according to the rank or zeal of his master; from ten to forty, or forty-five rupees monthly. He is considered as the head of the servants, having much respect paid him by the menials in general, and being permitted, by many of the more liberal students, to enter the apartments without taking off his shoes; an omission, for which the other servants would be severely punished, it implying the greatest contempt and disrespect.

As to the swarms of Moonshees who are retained in all the public departments, their wages are generally very low. Their dress is proportionately neglected, and they are by no means either so respectable, or so well informed. Their being thoroughly acquainted with the respective designations of the persons they are to address (a matter of wondrous jealousy among the natives, those of rank, in particular, whose titles often occupy nine-tenths of a long manuscript), and a free hand, together with a quick reading, are their best recommendations.

The Moonshee, attached to a gentleman studying the languages, generally has a boy to attend him; who, besides carrying his bundle of writing apparatus, holds the umbrella over his master, on his way to and from home. Many of these boys, by application and the indulgence of their masters, pick up a smattering of the Persian language, and learn to read and write sufficiently to be, in time, employed in offices. Some have been known to raise themselves into very comfortable and distinguished situations.

# PLATE II.

## A GENTLEMAN IN HIS PRIVATE OFFICE, ATTENDED BY HIS DUFTOREE, OR NATIVE OFFICE-KEEPER.

THE Duftoree is not an hereditary employment, nor is it confined to any particular religion or sect. Both Hindoos and Mussulmans are to be found in this capacity. The duty of the Duftoree requires much regularity and great circumspection. He must see that every part of the office be clean, the ink-stands filled, the desks properly arranged, the papers dusted; and, in general, all in readiness for the clerks. However, it must not be understood that the Duftoree sweeps the office floor; that being the exclusive duty of a menial kept for such purposes only. Were the Duftoree to submit to such a drudgery, he would become an outcast from among his own tribe, and be subjected to the most mortifying insults and heavy fines.

A good Duftoree should be expert at making pens and ruling books; and I have seen some who could bind books so as to be ready for being covered with leather. That part, however, not one will undertake; it being held as unclean, and considered the business of a particular sect, with whom it is hereditary. In fact, all operations in which leather is employed, must be done by those who are bôrn to the trade, and who are, in general, considered as defiled. Their very touch is offensive to those of the superior sects, who invariably perform either a partial or general ablution after contact with a worker in leather. These scruples, though still in force to a most inconvenient degree, certainly have dimished since Europeans have been in authority in India; and, at some remote period, may probably disappear.

The wages of a Duftoree are from four to six rupees monthly. Some gentlemen present their Duftorees with a livery, consisting of a turban and waist-band, of the same colour as those worn by their other domestics. The ends of both are in general tipped with some other colour for about a foot or more; and creates a distinction, whereby the equipage of most gentlemen may be known at a considerable distance.

III.

*London, Published & Sold by Edw^d Orme, March 1^st 1813.*

# PLATE III.

## A GENTLEMAN, IN A PUBLIC OFFICE, ATTENDED BY THE CRANNIES, OR NATIVE CLERKS.

THESE are employed in all the offices under government, and in the several mercantile firms throughout India. They are, with very few exceptions, Hindoos, and obtain situations merely from an ability to write a clear hand with tolerable quickness. It may appear strange, but it is perfectly true, that many Crannies, who can read and write English with fluency and correctness, do not understand one word in ten! Some of them are mere copyists, and are utterly ignorant as to the sense or purport of letters they transcribe in the highest style of penmanship. Others, again, affect great erudition, which they are desirous of displaying on all occasions. They pore over dictionaries until they think themselves perfectly finished. The following note, copied verbatim from the writing of one of these pedantic gentry, may serve to show with what success he had thumbed Johnson's Dictionary. It was written to inform his master of a window shutter having been blown off by a north-wester:

“ Honourable Sir,

“ Last night monstrous breeze come, make all house palpitate. Window shutter very much agitated; and, after much trepidation, relinquish from the frame, and subside to the ground. I make carpenter come to conjoin immediately. Mistress very great fright."

And nothing hurt the poor fellow more than being told what stuff he had written. He really believed his note to be the very achmé of literature!

Crannies write at desks with apparatus of every description, similar to what we use in our offices. Stationery, of all kinds, is exported to India in large quantities. The natives generally sit on the ground to write, using a reed pen, ink made of lamp-black, and paper made in the country either of cotton, bamboo, or other materials, indigenous throughout India.

The Bengallies, for the most part, wear white clothes: they have a dotee, or cloth, wrapped round their waists, reaching to their calves, and sometimes one end thrown over their shoulders. The turban is small and compact; frequently open at the top, and allowing a small lock of long hair, tied in a knot, to hang through the opening The Hindoos shave their heads quite bare, except the lock in question, which may occupy about an inch in diameter, and is left just over the summit of the brain. To bereave a Hindoo of this remnant would irritate him to an extreme, and cause him to seek the most determined and cruel revenge.

IIII.

London Published & Sold by Edw.d Orme, March 1st 1813.

# PLATE IV.

## A GENTLEMAN DRESSING, ATTENDED BY HIS HEAD-BEARER, AND OTHER SERVANTS.

A Gentleman is here seen reading, while a servant washes his feet in a large vessel, made either of tutanag, copper, or brass, but generally the former; this may be about four inches deep, and from fifteen to eighteen in diameter. It has a broad rim like a plate, to which a strainer of corresponding metal is fitted, and may be removed at pleasure. This strainer is essential to comfort, as it conceals the water soiled by washing the hands, &c. the water being poured by a servant from an ewer, for the most part tutenag, or from an earthen *soorie*, or jug. A servant is seen holding a towel in readiness to dry the foot so soon as washed. It should be observed, that the balosoro-bearers, who in a manner monopolize that occupation in and about Calcutta, will not touch a chillumchee, or washing vessel, under pretence of being defiled, should they come in contact with the impurities washed from the skin of a Christian. And this prejudice (which is a famous tool in the hands of these crafty, lazy fellows,) extends so far, that the man who will pour the water from the ewer, will not, on any account, touch a chillumchee, even in the purest state of cleanliness. Similar customs and pleas, founded on religious tenets or antient usage, prevail throughout all classes of the natives.

Europeans, throughout India, sleep in long drawers, made of thin calico, on mattresses: the beds are, during the cold season, furnished with curtains of chintz, &c. and, at all times, inner curtains are used, made of *kabbradool*, which is a kind of gauze, manufactured from the refuse of raw silk, commonly dyed of a light green. These keep out the musquitos, which else in many parts of the country, especially in marshy situations, are very numerous, and cruelly troublesome. At Calcutta they may be heard, towards sun-set, swarming into the houses of Europeans, in full chorus, humming as loud as a stocking-weaver's loom. The natives but rarely cook their victuals before that time, when the smoke drives away the musquitos; then, getting on the wing, they throng towards the quarter occupied by Europeans principally.

Such gentlemen as take exercise on horseback, rise with the first glimpse of the dawn, and return as the sun gets above the horizon. A glass of water, cooled by means of pewter bottles agitated in a solution of saltpetre, is drank by most gentlemen before breakfast. Its effects are very salutary: few who adhere to this custom fail of a good appetite, or are much troubled with bile. The general practice of having four or five large pots of cold water thrown over the head, either in the morning or before dressing for dinner, is not less efficacious in regard to bracing the muscles; and prevents that dreadful relaxation, to which persons are subject in hot climates.

IV.

London, Published & Sold by Edwd. Orme, March 1st 1813.

# PLATE V.

## A GENTLEMAN ATTENDED BY HIS HAJAUM, OR NATIVE BARBER.

The Hajaum, or Barber, is often a menial, receiving three or four rupees monthly, and attending at stated hours at his master's residence, having the rest of the day to himself. Those in the employ of the Europeans, are more cleanly and expert than the common village tonsors; who shave with a razor fixed to a piece of wood, and having a blade in shape somewhat similar to a hatchet. They are not very nice about the quality of their soap, which usually has a most offensive smell. Among such as officiate for the natives only, a brush is not to be expected: the face is previously moistened with water, rubbed on with the hand; after which, a lump of fœtid soap being applied in the same handy way, a lather is raised, and the operator, totally regardless of the wincing and significant looks of the suffering customer, coolly removes, not only the beard, but often a large portion of the skin. It has frequently been my lot to submit, through positive necessity, to this dreadful havock; and to find, that at least a week or ten days were needful, to repair the damage done to my chin!

The natives have their ears pricked with a small steel instrument; at the other end of which is a kind of chissel, about a line in breadth, wherewith the Barbers pare their nails very dexterously, first moistening them with water. These instruments are usually very sharp, and well set; at least, far better than the hatchet razors, which are not very delicately applied to the grindstone, and finished on a piece of cow hide, an old shoe-sole, or whatever may offer to the indifferent Hajaum. A small looking-glass of perhaps two inches square, however, is furnished; not very fine in quality, but faithful enough to convince the poor man who has been shaved, that his feelings were by no means inconsistent with the appearance of his visage.

It is likewise considered a part of the Hajaum's duty to supple the joints by pulling, twisting, and other modes not very acceptable to Europeans, but much relished by the natives. I was once surprised by an active adept in this branch; who, putting his razor into his mouth, suddenly gave my head such a twist, as made me doubt whether I should ever look straight again; and occasioned me to be very cautious in prohibiting strange Hajaums from a similar indulgence in so painful a luxury!

V.

London, Published & Sold by Edw.d Orme. March 1.st 1803.

# PLATE VI.

## A GENTLEMAN DELIVERING A LETTER TO A SOONTAH-BURDAR, OR SILVER BATON-BEARER.

THIS is a servant retained only by persons of rank, or in office: he bears a short silver *baton*, of about two feet long, rather thicker at the upper end, where it is ordinarily a little curved, like the handle of a hanger, and is ornamented with a tiger's face, or some such device; the other end is considerably smaller. These batons are formed of solid silver cases, filled with rosin, the same as many of our knives and forks.

The *Soontah-Burdar*, literally implying the stick-bearer, is next in rank to the *Chobe-Dhar*, or pole-bearer: the latter has a straight pole, of similar formation, about five feet long, and from three to four inches diameter at the top, tapering down to about an inch and a half at the bottom, where it is armed with a strong ferrule of iron, or other substantial metal. Some persons of distinction retain both these classes of servants, which, not only attend at the hall doors, to announce guests, and to deliver or receive notes and messages, but attend the palankeen, by the side of which they run; observing that they hold precedence in so doing, according to their proximity to the person of their master or mistress; the other parts of the retinue preceding the palankeen in the same order, as far as relates to rank. There is sometimes a *Jemmadar*, or head servant, who bears no insignia of the foregoing descriptions; but who, being either a confidential or old servant, proceeds at the side of the machine, probably in conversation with his employer.

The wages of these superior servants vary much in different parts of the country. A *Jemmadar* may receive from about twelve to thirteen rupees monthly; a *Chobe-Dhar*, from eight to fifteen; and a *Soontah-Burdar*, from five to ten; but much depends on the number of persons thus retained. They generally wear belts of coloured cloth, bordered in a showy manner, and a breastplate of silver or brass, with the initials of their master's names. Many have liveries, not only in respect to their turbans and waistbands, but likewise corresponding vests of perpet, or some good woollen stuff.

All this tribe of servants, who are in general Mahometans, take their origin from the more menial capacity of *Hircarrah*, or messenger; and, in the first instance, bear nothing but a walking-stick, having a cotton tassel, and armed with an iron spike. *Piadas*, or *Peons*, literally implying footmen, though, in most respects, of the same occupation as the *Hircarrahs*, carry no stick. *Peons* are ordinarily employed by persons in business for their correspondence, &c.

within the places they reside at; whereas, *Hircarrahs* are often sent immense distances: they carry the posts, which every where are conveyed by footmen; who, including all stops, proceed at the rate of about four miles within the hour; making their stages with as much exactness, in regard to time, in fair weather, as our mails.

VI.

London, Published & Sold by Edwd. Orme, March 1st 1813.

VIII.

London, Published & Sold by Edw.d Orme, March 1.st 1813.

# PLATE VII.

## A GENTLEMAN'S KEDMUTGARS, OR TABLE SERVANTS, BRINGING IN DINNER.

THESE are servants particularly employed in preparing all the apparatus for breakfast, dinner, &c. and they occasionally assist in the kitchen. It should be observed, that women are never employed in any domestic situation, except in the *zenònah*, or women's apartments, into which men are never supposed to obtain admission. One or more *Kedmutgars* invariably attends each gentleman at table, during the hot season; and, when flies are troublesome, all are provided with small hand *punkahs*, or fans, or with whisks made of hair, feathers, or grass roots. Each *Kedmutgar* stands behind his master's chair, and supplies him with every thing he may require.

Very few but Mussulmans are to be found in this capacity; the occupation being such as to disgust Hindoos, who are particularly enjoined by their religion not to touch poultry, nor to kill any animal whatever; consequently they are incapable of a thousand duties to which *Kedmutgars* are subject. Many are excellent confectioners and cooks, and rise to the superior distinction of *Khansammah*, or head of the household; and, in lieu of receiving only from five to eight rupees monthly, often obtain twenty, or even thirty rupees wages.

*Mosaulebees*, or torch-bearers, often by long services, or peculiar merit; perhaps, too, by means of a forged certificate, of having served as *Kedmutgars*, often obtain that rank. But, in general, vacancies are supplied from among the sons of *Ayas*, or nurses; who, through the interest of their mistresses, obtain situations for their effeminate offspring, who, in due time, become as complete puppies and loungers in their way, as can be found among the lackies of Europe! Many of them are however very excellent, steady, and clever servants, remarkable for fidelity and attachment: instances can be adduced of their living with gentlemen for upwards of twenty years, attending them to every quarter of India, and eventually to Europe!

VIII.

London. Published & Sold by Edwd. Orme. March 1st 1813.

# PLATE VIII.

## AN ENGLISH FAMILY AT TABLE, UNDER A PŪNKAH, OR FAN, KEPT IN MOTION BY A KHELASSY.

Those who serve under this designation may be divided into various classes; some being in the employ of gentlemen, others appertaining more to the military, especially the artillery department; and some being trained entirely to naval purposes. Though all are to be found occasionally under the circumstances described in the annexed Plate, yet we must rather confine our ideas to the *Khelassy* retained in the service of European gentlemen for the purposes of attending upon camp-equipage, pitching and striking tents, with various other occupations in which this class of servants mix with other menials. In point of utility and readiness, the *Khelassy* is, perhaps, inferior to none. They receive from four to six rupees monthly, and ordinarily are provided with a jacket of some dark-coloured perpet, with contrasted facings; wearing blue turbans and waistbands, with white under-vests, and drawers of the same, or of striped gingham. A piece of red tape, or list, goes round the edge of the turban, which is, for the most part, formed the same as those in use among the *Sepoy* regiments.

The *Khelassies* in the military service are very numerous, and are organized in regular companies, in which they rise to superior ranks, in the same manner as in the *Sepoy* corps. They are inexpressibly useful in the ordnance branch; drawing the cannon, and performing all the duties which would prove too severe for Europeans in so adverse a climate.

This Plate describes a *Khelassy* swinging a large *Punkah*, or fan; which, being suspended from the top of the room, by means of several strong cords, or by iron hooks, is drawn to and fro, by the man who has hold of a rope which communicates with the *Punkah*, and to which it is fastened in two or more places. The *Punkah* consists of a light frame, of such length as may suit the room, perhaps fifteen feet long, and four in depth, covered with chintz, or coloured linen: being set in motion, it agitates the air greatly, and affords extreme refreshment to such as are seated under its line of action. Persons unaccustomed to the *Punkah*, sometimes are attacked with head-aches, which, however, in general, gradually become less troublesome, after being habituated to the use of this very agreeable and highly useful machine. Care should be taken to examine the ropes, by which the *Punkah* is suspended, from time to time; as many have fallen in consequence of their action cutting through the ropes. Though I have witnessed several accidents of this kind, I do not recollect ever seeing any person hurt; the damage has generally been limited to a few dishes, glasses, &c. being broken, or a table defaced.

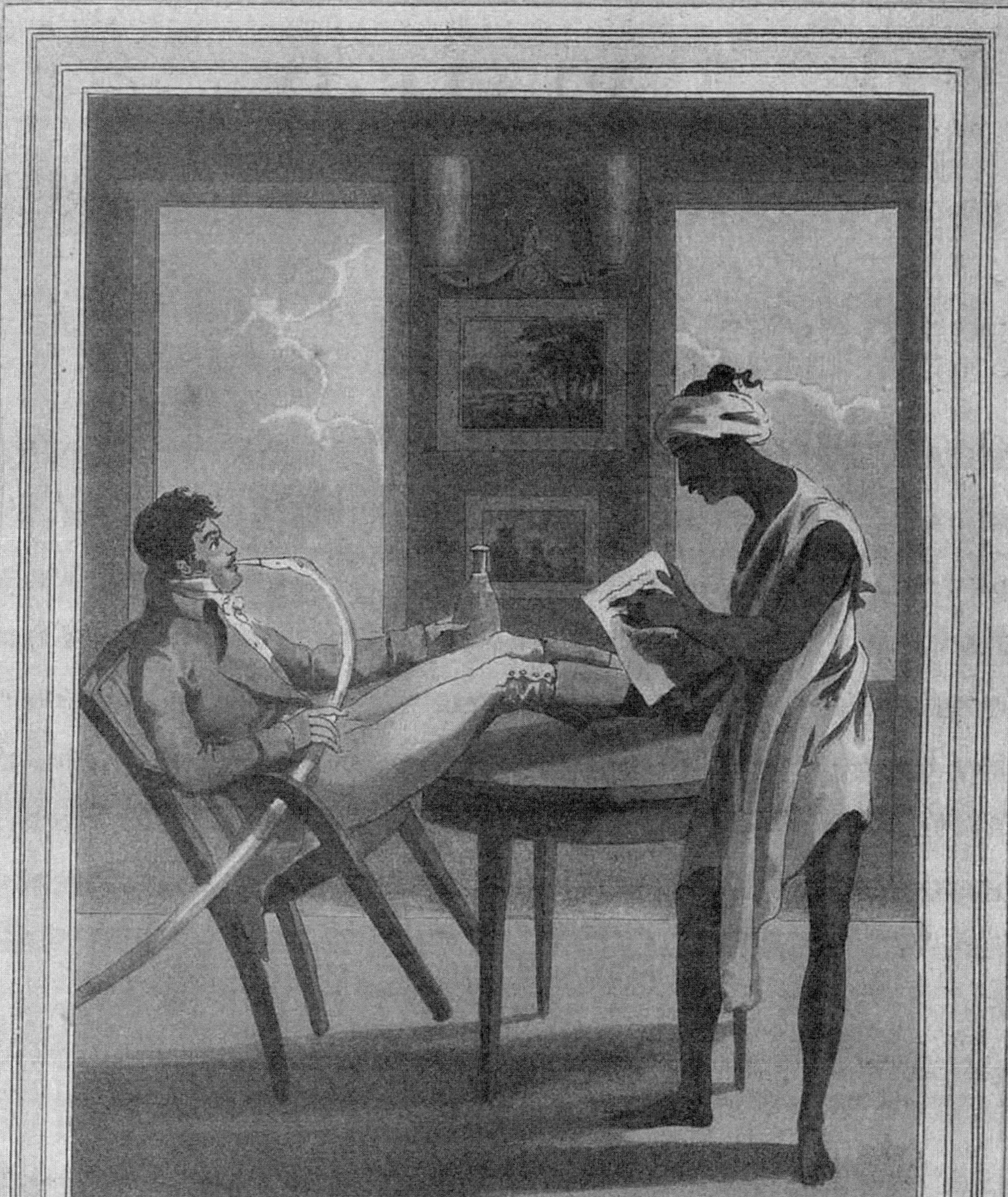

IX.

London, Published & Sold by Edwd. Orme, March 1st 1813.

# PLATE IX.

## A GENTLEMAN WITH HIS SIRCAR, OR MONEY-SERVANT.

It is devoutly to be hoped, that this very numerous and formidable gang of public and private dependers may speedily become extinct. To persons unacquainted with the customs of the natives of rank, and of the practices among Europeans some twenty years back, it might appear wonderful how such a race of miscreants obtained a footing among either. It would be going too far out of my limits were I to enter on a minute description; and, indeed, it may suffice generally to state, that these money-dealers were formerly in too general employ. Gentlemen in India rarely or never carry money in their pockets, except when travelling; and, until lately, each retained in his service a *Sircar*, whose business was to make all purchases, and to receive and disburse all monies.

The necessity of such a servant was first imputable to the great variety of coins, with the value and distinction of which they were supposed to be infallibly, and, in a manner, exclusively intimate; though the *Podars* are really the only connoisseurs in this difficult branch of business. The mints established by the Honourable East India Company, at their several presidencies and subordinate residences, however, diminished this obstacle so much, by simplifying the ordinary concerns in money, as to enable the generality of servants to receive and pay without great danger of loss. This reduced the importance of the *Sircars* greatly: however, they yet hold their posts in all public offices, and in the houses of merchants, &c. of extensive dealings.

The pay of these locusts, who are all Hindoos, may be from ten to thirty rupees monthly; but with many the salary is scarcely an object. Nay, some serve without pay, in consequence of the customary fees and various perquisites they continue to obtain. *Sircars*, as before observed, are in general employed to purchase whatever their masters may want; and, as the venders always allow what is called *dustoory*, or the customary deduction of a sixteenth to the *Sircar*, it may be reasonably supposed, that the latter does not always go to the cheapest market; unless, indeed, he may charge more than the *dustoory* would amount to.

*Sircars*, frequently after arriving at a certain state of real opulence, or credit, become *Shroffs*, or money-brokers, and carry on very extensive concerns throughout India. They raise or depress the exchange between various cities in a most summary manner. Often a traveller finds, to his cost, that two places, within thirty or forty miles, mutually depreciate each other's coin; perhaps to the extent of fifteen or twenty per cent. Nay, such is the contrivance, and such the impudence of the *Shroffs* of Calcutta, that they arbitrarily change the value, even of the lawful gold and currency, ten or twelve per cent.! This is done daily, more or less, under the eye of the government, which has not, we presume, as yet, been able to put an adequate check to the nocturnal meetings of the *Shroffs;* who, after the business of the day is over, meet and fix the exchange between the several cities, the current value of the gold and silver coins, and the premium or discount the government securities are to bear on the following day.

The importance and peculiar circumstances inseparably attached to this article have forced me to some prolixity; yet I hope the indulgent reader will allow me to add, that, until some means be applied, adequate to the evil I have described, not only individuals, but the Honourable Company, must be very great sufferers from the depredations of these leagued villains. It need hardly be stated, that all contractors take especial care to cover themselves, in their calculations, from the loss to which they must else be subject; consequently that loss must ultimately fall on the government.

With regard to dress, the *Sircars* may be classed with the *Keramies*, or clerks, many of whom act occasionally as money-servants.

X.

London Published & Sold by Edw.d Orme, March 1st 1813.

# PLATE X.

## A GENTLEMAN WITH HIS HOOKAH-BURDAR, OR PIPE-BEARER.

THE *Hookah*, or pipe, is in general use among the natives of rank and opulence: it was also nearly as universally retained among Europeans. Time, however, has retrenched this very costly luxury so much, that not one in three now smokes. Many are absolutely slaves to their *Hookahs;* which, excepting while sleeping, or in the early parts of meals, are ever at hand. This fascinating enjoyment seems with some to be indispensably necessary to happiness, though I never yet could reconcile myself to its use; and have ever found those, who were most bigotted to smoking, the greatest dupes to their *Hookah Burdars*, or preparers of the Pipe, who imposed on their masters the most nauseating mundungus under the high sounding title of *Bilsah Tobacco!* The truth, is, that the small village of *Bilsah*, situate in the *Maharatta* country, does not produce above a twentieth part of the tobacco sold under that designation. The name, however, raises the price, and enables the vender, and the *Hookah-Burdar*, to derive handsome profits in their dealings with Europeans for this celebrated article.

The office of *Hookah-Burdar* is common both to Hindoos and Mussulmans, though more prevalent among the latter. The dress is the same as that of the *Kedmutgars*, many of whom occasionally attend at table, and prepare the *Hookah*. The wages are generally from six to ten rupees monthly; many receive much more: indeed, I have heard more than one gentleman boast, that their smoking expenses did not come within an hundred rupees. Some even keep two *Hookah-Burdars*, to attend them by night as well as by day.

The *Hookah* apparatus consists of the glass, or composition bottom, equal to about two quarts, which should be two-thirds filled with clear cold water. The snake, or pliant tube, is about ten feet long, made of a particular kind of bark, resembling that of the plane, or sycamore, bound round a skeleton of pewter wire, and ultimately covered with calico and *cobbradool*, generally black or purple. At one end a mouth-piece of agate, or composition, fixes on a small wooden socket, and the other end fastens by the like means to a bamboo tube, which joins to another that is immersed in the water about three inches: on this last, which rises a foot or more perpendicularly, stands an earthen receiver, which supports a piece of tile, or *towah*, having on its bottom the tobacco, made into a cake by means of molasses, plantains, &c. This tile is kept a little above the edge of the receiver, or *chillum*, so that the air may draw freely through the water into the empty part of the *Hookah* bottom. On the *towah*, or tile, four half balls of a kind of charcoal, peculiarly prepared from burnt rice, are placed, red hot; these cause a smoke to arise from the tobacco on the bottom of the *towah*. A silver ornament, called a *surpoos*, or cover, is placed over the *gools*, or hot balls, adorned with chains, and curiously carved or filigreed; its bottom rests on the upper rim of the *chillum*, or receiver. As it is necessary to wash the *nichah*, or snake, daily on a horse-hair rope, and that, unless wet, the smoke does not draw easily, a cloth is generally wrapped on that part near the mouth-piece, which is held by the person smoking, and reaching far enough down the snake, to keep his clothes from being soiled or damped.

The heat of the climate is such, during eight months of the year, as to require that all beverages be cooled by means of saltpetre; and such wine as is placed in bottles on the table, (for decanters are very seldom used) is invariably covered with bags of *curroah*, or other cloth, kept constantly wet. The free and easy practice of putting the legs on the table is yet adopted by many, though the *moorah*, a kind of hassock, made for that purpose, is now in general use. It may be deemed an effeminate luxury; but experience sanctions as essential, what custom has rendered familiar. The want of a *moorah*, or some substitute, for raising the legs and feet to an horizontal position, is always felt most severely by every old inhabitant of India.

XI.

London, Published & Sold by Edwd. Orme March 1st 1813.

# PLATE XI.

## A SAUMPAREEAH, OR SNAKE-CATCHER, EXHIBITING SNAKES BEFORE EUROPEANS.

It is impossible to describe the various kinds of Snakes, which are to be found throughout India, in this limited Work. An ample account of them may be found in the "Wild Sports of India," published by the Editor of this Volume. Suffice it to say, that, for the most part, the Land Snakes are highly venomous, often causing almost instantaneous death. In the Work alluded to, the reputed antidotes are treated of, and the *Jehneuneon*, which is the inveterate foe of all the Serpent tribe, is particularly described. The Snake-Catcher heeds not the size of the reptile he is to secure; all being subject either to his great agility, or to the various devices in use. Thus we see that immense animal, the *Adjghur*, which often measures from twenty to near thirty feet in length; and, in thickness, equal to the body of a moderate-sized man, exhibited by the *Saumpareeah*, and obeying him with tolerable exactness.

With regard to the venom of Snakes in general, its mode of communication at the time of biting, its effects, and other circumstances connected therewith, the reader is referred to "The Wild Sports of India," it being incompatible with the present undertaking to enlarge on points of Natural History.

Snakes are usually carried in flat circular baskets, with close covers, all made of rattans, or of close wicker-work. Of course they vary in size, according to the bulk of the reptiles to be conveyed. One *Bangy-wallah*, or bearer of an equipoised sling, will usually convey some dozens of Snakes. But I have seen some so large as to require a cart to convey them: indeed, I recollect seeing one *Adjghur*, which required eight men to lift him. He, however, by dint of practice, very familiarly ascended into his basket, which was not removed from the carriage. These unwieldy monsters do not seem to be at all affected by the music of a rude kind of hautboy, on which one of the *Saumpareeahs* performs while the Snakes are exhibiting; but the smaller sorts, especially the *Covra-Capella*, rears to a great height, on hearing the instrument; and, being kept in attention by the show-man, may be said to dance to the music; though, strictly speaking, it acts but according to its natural habits, on being opposed, face to face, to any other animal.

The constant fatigue to which the Snakes are subject, added to the tenderness, no doubt, occasioned by the extraction of the poisonous fangs, renders them extremely passive, and embolden the exhibitor to handle them without any apparent fear. However, I have seen some of the large ones not only bite so severely as to occasion much bleeding; but, by their writhings round the *Saumpareeah's* cheek, arms, and legs, give very uncomfortable squeezes, causing him to grin with obvious sincerity.

# PLATE XII.

## MARQUIS WELLESLEY'S DANDY, OR BOATMAN, IN HIS LIVERY.

THE person exhibited in this Plate must not be viewed as the ordinary *Dandy*, or boatman, employed in the vessels trading throughout the country; these being generally poor naked wretches, whose avocation is, perhaps, the most laborious of any yet known, and whose depravity and thievish habits are absolutely proverbial. The uniform in which the subject of this Chapter is habited, is the distinguishing dress of the boatmen employed by Marquis Wellesley, the late Governor General of India, on board the Honourable Company's State Yacht, the *Soonamooky*, and its attendant *Pheel-Cherrah*, or light barge, the head of which is ornamented, or rather constructed, with the resemblance of the fore parts of an Elephant; whence its designation. The *Soonamooky*, implying "the appearance of gold," was built by Mr. Hastings, while Governor, of teak wood, sheathed with copper, and was fitted up in a style suited to the dignity of a Viceroy. If my memory serves me right, this vessel, which is a strange mixture of European and oriental naval architecture, cost no less than forty-five thousand rupees. It can row about thirty oars; but, from its great size and heavy construction, it requires the aid of many tow-boats to enable its making any great progress, though I understand it tracks and sails extremely well.

Though, on great occasions, a display of rich livery may be necessary, and that the wearer, no doubt, may feel all the consequence attached to his station; yet, excepting in very cold days, a thick woollen vest must prove highly obnoxious to a person labouring at the oar; especially with that energy, inseparable from the pride of superior dignity and exerted emulation! In the *Pheel-Cherrahs*, and other smaller boats, the *Dandies* row either with oars, or paddles, such as are used in canoes. The latter are particularly useful in narrow creeks, such as abound in the *Sunderbund*, where often, for miles together, it would be impossible to use oars. Many *Pheel-Cherrahs* and *Moheer Punkies*, which are of the same construction, and vary only in having a Peacock instead of an Elephant's head, row from thirty to fifty oars, and proceed at the rate of ten or twelve miles within the hour. They, however, cannot enter into competition with snakes, so called from their form; which, being perhaps sixty or seventy feet long, and not more than three broad, absolutely dart through the water, when well manned, as they generally are, having as many *Dandies* on board as they can accommodate. Exclusive of the danger of upsetting, this class of boats is peculiarly ineligible, on account of the numerous eddies in the great rivers, wherein they frequently snap about the middle, and sink without a moment's warning.

XII.

London Published & Sold by Edw.d Orme, March 1st 1813.

# PLATE XIII.

## AN EUROPEAN LADY GIVING INSTRUCTIONS TO HER DURZEE, OR NATIVE TAILOR.

THE dress of Europeans being so very different from that of the natives, and a large stock of linen being necessary for the purpose of shifting twice in the day, occasion the necessity for every family, indeed for every individual, to retain a tailor in the house. They are all men, and receive wages in proportion to their ability. They find their own thread; which is very fine cotton, spun into small bundles. At least a quarter of every tailor's time is occupied in twisting four or five threads together, it being too slight to bear any stress singly. A *Durzee* in the employ of a bachelor, where there is no extraordinary work to do, beyond cutting out, making and repairing the linen of his master and his lady behind the curtain, usually receives from five to eight rupees monthly. Such as are capable of making ladies' dresses are in great requisition, and often receive extraordinary wages: I have known them as high as thirty rupees!

Being always in the house, and generally very neat in their dresses, as also having to measure the ladies occasionally, in particular for various articles required to fit them about the neck and body with great exactness, affords the *Durzees* a thousand opportunities for intrigue; of which, it is generally believed, they are rarely disinclined to profit. They are great cheats as to the quantity of cloth required to make up the articles wanted; and, when they are allowed to value the linens while purchasing, or to stand as interpreters between their masters and the *Buzzazes*, or cloth merchants, never fail to put themselves on a good footing with the latter; who, exclusive of the *dustoory*, or customary sixteenth, privately recompense the *honest* mediator, for his conscientious discharge of duty towards his employer.

The dress of the tailor is much the same as that of the *Kedmutgar*, from whom, however, he appears as distinct as the brethren of the thimble do among us. All mechanics and artisans, throughout India, invariably work on the ground; benches and shop-boards are unknown. The measures used by the *Durzees* are made of cloth, having the divisions marked by threads of opposite colours. Many of them work quick, and with wonderful neatness. The *Durzees*, who make regimentals, &c. generally confine themselves to coat making; and, are now becoming so numerous and expert, as well as so cheap, as to preclude the possibility for European tailors to obtain a livelihood, where formerly they used to make princely fortunes!

XIII.

London, Published & Sold by Edwd. Orme, March 1st 1813.

# PLATE XIV.

## A DANCING WOMAN, OF BENGAL, EXHIBITING BEFORE AN EUROPEAN FAMILY.

A WIDE distinction exists between the dancing women of Bengal Proper, and those of the Upper Provinces: the latter are in the greater estimation among Europeans. Not, indeed, that much can be said by this meretricious tribe in general. The beauty of individuals, and the grace with which they dance, or accompany their songs, usually establishes the fame of the set to which they appertain. For the greater portion are either slaves, bought by adventurous bawds, during times of scarcity; or are deluded girls, that have been seduced from their families at a very early age; probably, when only five or six years old, and trained up to this infamous calling.

We must not, however, estimate reputation on the same scale by which it is valued among us. The immense number of young women retained among the natives in their *harams*, or seraglios, as well as the common practice among Europeans of having native housekeepers, renders that desultory cohabitude, so much condemned among European nations, rather enviable than infamous. Such women as are celebrated for perfection in this line, often rise to very important situations, and eventually leave their posterity to rank with the greatest families in the country.

They all dance barefooted, on a kind of carpet, called *satringe*, having on a pair of drawers, either of a rich cloth, called *gool-budden*, or of *keemkob:* a loose vest of fine calico, with only two or three inches of sleeve, and reaching down half way from the hip to the knee, is all the body clothing they wear; but a large *dooputtah*, resembling a plaid in form and size, made of fine muslin, bordered with a broad band of silk, is thrown over the head, and falls negligently over the shoulders. The grace with which this part of the dress is managed, constitutes much of the dancer's merit. The *peishwauz* is a small bodied gown, made extremely full, and gathered up close to the bosom, reaching to the ankles, and having sleeves down to the wrists. This is worn on all public occasions, and gives the dancer great scope to exhibit her management. The hair is divided in the middle, and flattened down with a mercilage made from steeped linseed. The forehead of the Bengal women is generally painted with vermilion, or ground sandal wood. The ears, nose, neck, arms, wrists, ankles, toes, and fingers, are amply furnished with trinkets; but in far less profusion than among the women of the Upper Provinces.

The apartment described in this Plate, represents the Interior of the House of a rich Native of Calcutta, named *Sookma Roy*, a person remarkable for many excellent qualities, especially for his attachment and hospitality towards Europeans.

XIV.

London, Published & Sold by Edwd. Orme, March 1st. 1813.

# PLATE XV.

## A DANCING WOMAN, OF LUEKNOW, EXHIBITING BEFORE AN EUROPEAN FAMILY.

LUEKNOW being the capital of the Nabob Vizier of Oude, at whose court all the luxuries of the East abound, and where most of the rich natives have either a residence or an agent, that city naturally becomes the resort of such persons as are celebrated in their several callings, or who possess a liberal spirit of adventure. Accordingly, we find many *tuffahs*, or sets of dancing girls, at Lueknow, eminent either for their personal charms, or the superior elegance of their accomplishments. The natives, however, are not so liberal to these Cyprian devotees as formerly; nor indeed, all things considered, do they, by any means, retain the splendour and munificence which, some years back, were their peculiar characteristics. The people of Hindostan have undergone a change of character, within the last thirty years, in consequence of the introduction of Europeans and their customs, among the superior classes of the natives. Whether from that circumstance, or the great influx of young officers, &c. that arrived from Europe, between the years 1778 and 1785, it is certain, that the prime sets of dancing girls quitted the cities, and repaired to the several cantonments, where they met the most liberal encouragement. Then the celebrated *Kaunum* was in the zenith of her glory! Those who did not witness the dominion she held over a numerous train of abject followers, would never credit, that a haughty, ugly, filthy, black woman, could, solely by the grace of her motions, and the novelty of some Cashmerian airs, hold in complete subjection, and render absolutely tributary, many scores of fine young British officers! Nay, even the more discreet and experienced, many of whom could not, with propriety, say, "Time has not thinned my flowing hair, nor bent me with his iron hand," were found among the most fervent of the proud *Kaunum*'s admirers. Reason, however, rode post on the wings of military retrenchment, and the Auditor-General's red ink negatives dissolved the charm. *Kaunum* retired, and the various sets of inferior consideration speedily sunk into neglect.

The women of the Upper Provinces are generally much fairer than those of Bengal Proper. They also wear more ornaments; they dance with more precision; though not, in general, with such wanton gestures as the latter; who certainly, in the opinion of the *oldest* judges, accompany the *caharwah*, or fandango of India, with such meretricious action, as decidedly gives them the claim to unparalleled immodesty!!!

It should be understood, that the dancing women of India pique themselves entirely on the gracefulness of their positions and motions. They have no variety of steps, the feet being kept parallel and close; one foot advancing, or moving only a few inches, and the other always following it: this, however, is done with remarkable exactness as to time, which, on all occasions, is regulated by the instruments played by men attached to the set. Many of the songs and airs are highly interesting; and the band, who play by rote, are extremely exact in their accompaniments. This diversion is now nearly obsolete among Europeans; a circumstance by no means discreditable, nor to be regretted.

XV.

*London. Published & Sold. by Edwd. Orme, March 1st 1813.*

XVI.

London, Published & Sold by Edw.d Orme. March 1st 1813.

# PLATE XVI.

## AN EUROPEAN LADY, ATTENDED BY A SERVANT USING A HAND PUNKAH, OR FAN.

THERE are various kinds and sizes of the hand *Punkah*. The largest are such as we generally find accompany palankeens, being carried by one of the bearers in lieu of an umbrella. These are formed of a staff about five feet long, near the end of which, a circular frame, of perhaps twenty-eight or thirty inches diameter, is affixed to the side, forming somewhat the shape of the letter P. The frame is covered with any coloured or printed calico, on both sides, and is furnished with a very full flounce, all the way round, of about a foot or more in depth, of the same stuff. The staves are lackered generally in broad rings, of various colours, strongly contrasted.

Other *Punkahs* are made from the branches of the *palmirah*, or toddy tree; which, being very large and solid, answer this purpose admirably. The leaf, which is crimped exactly like a lady's fan when half open, grows upon a very substantial branch, which, being split, forms an excellent handle or staff. Thus a *Punkah* may be made of any size, with the singular advantage of the whole being but one piece. The smaller kinds are literally hand *Punkahs*, they being waved to and fro by any person at pleasure. The larger sorts, which may be classed with those first noticed, require both hands to carry them, as a shelter against the sun or rain; for which purpose they are, however, very incompetent, when compared with a *chattah*, or umbrella.

Being rested on the ground, so that the lower end serves as a pivot, the larger kind of *Punkah* affords considerable refreshment, when swung backwards and forwards, by a servant. As they can be placed, in any situation, at pleasure, their convenience is greater, but their general use less, than that of the large suspended frame; which, of course, may be suspended as a fixture. The small hand *Punkahs* are extremely useful at night, during the very hot months; when persons waking, in consequence of the intense heat, are greatly relieved by their use. Few are without one at hand: indeed, I had once a very small frame *Punkah* suspended within my bed-curtains, which moved by means of a cord passing through them into another room. The pleasure and benefit I derived from it, causes me to wonder the plan did not become general.

XVII.

London. Published & Sold by Edw.d Orme. March 1st 1813.

# PLATE XVII.

## AN EUROPEAN LADY AND HER FAMILY, ATTENDED BY AN AYAH, OR NURSE.

THIS occupation is generally followed by such as, in the first instance, become wet nurses to the children of European ladies, who always avoid rearing them personally, on account of the extreme relaxation and peculiar inconvenience, to which they would else be subject. No children are put out to nurse: the *Dhood-Dhye*, or wet nurse, is invariably accommodated in the house, where she assumes no small degree of consequence, especially if she thinks her services indispensable. In the course of time she becomes one of the family, and changes from wet to dry nurse. Many of these women, whose first entrance into the service of Europeans is quite accidental, retain their situations for a great many years, and amass very comfortable independencies.

The *Ayahs* are commonly fond of children, as indeed the native women in general are; and this is not to be wondered at, for that attachment is a principal source of amusement. A total deficiency of education, the absence of every kind of rational recreation, except the game of *patcheess*, which is highly interesting, and possesses all the intricacy of backgammon, without its noise, compels the *Ayahs* into that habit of endearment and attention, which renders them far better calculated for the care of children, than our juvenile race of nurses, whose time is commonly divided between the novel and the window seat!

*Ayahs* generally wear but one piece of cloth to serve as a petticoat and *dooputtah.* This being wrapped round their waists, and puckered up, is secured, and the residue is thrown over the head; to bare which is considered, among the women of Hindostan, as highly indecent. This cloth, which may be about five yards long, and broad enough to reach from the waist nearly to the ankles, is generally of white, with a coloured border; or is wove in stripes or checkers of various colours; among which, blue and a dirty red are most prevalent. A *koortah*, or thin vest of muslin, completes the dress. The wages of this class, which may be either Mahometan or Hindoo, ordinarily extend from four to eight rupees monthly; their duty is confined entirely to nursing and attending children; which, however, are always sent to Europe, when four or five years old, for education.

XVIII.

London. Published & Sold by Edwd. Orme. March 1st 1813.

# PLATE XVIII.

## KAUT-POOTLIES, OR PUPPETS, EXHIBITED BY NATIVE JUGGLERS, FOR THE AMUSEMENT OF EUROPEAN CHILDREN.

The Jugglers of India stand acknowledged, by all who have seen them, as the most complete of their profession: their several legerdemain tricks, exclusive of some astonishing feats peculiar to themselves, are managed with such adroitness, as could not fail to call forth the approbation of even our most celebrated exhibitors! Their puppet-shows possess more humour than our's, and are managed with more regularity and neatness. A sort of booth is erected, having a theatrical front and stage for the display of the *Kaut-pootlies*, literally implying "wooden infant." The operators, for there are generally two or more, are concealed behind a cloth, over which they direct the movements of the puppets, and give vocal imitations suited to the representation, in which the devices of thieves never fail to bear a principal share.

No people in the world are better calculated to give a faithful idea, of all that relates to furtive operations, than the Jugglers; they being commonly notorious thieves, who, under the cloak of displaying their ingenuity, especially among the inhabitants of the *zenonah*, take advantage of their admission to survey the premises and the effects, so as to steal them during the night. It would occupy folios to enumerate all the tricks that have been played off by this itinerant race of villains: suffice it to say, that in contrivance, boldness, and activity, they fairly distance our most expert sharpers and house-breakers.

Whatever be exhibited, whether the *Kaut-pootly*, gymnastic exercises, or legerdemain tricks, the *Tom-tom*, or drum, is an incessant accompaniment; its music is certainly not very inviting, but its beat serves to collect a crowd of all descriptions; who sometimes, on returning to their avocations, find that the light-fingered part of the gang, have not neglected to avail themselves of the absence of many, who unsuspectingly flew to the rendezvous, without duly securing their property.

I cannot close this subject, without remarking on the very extraordinary circumstance of many of the Jugglers, in India, passing the blades of swords, about twenty inches by two, down their throats, up to the very hilts. In this there is no deception: the fact is indisputable, and well known to thousands of Europeans; who, in spite of what is objected by surgical sceptics, have repeatedly witnessed it.

XIX.

London, Published & Sold by Edw.d Orme, March 1st 1813.

# PLATE XIX.

## A NATIVE GENTLEMAN SMOKING A GOORGOORY, OR HOOKAH, IN HIS PRIVATE APARTMENTS, ATTENDED BY HIS DANCING GIRLS

THE *Goorgoory* is formed on the same principles as the *Hookah;* but, for the sake of convenience, has, in lieu of a long pliant snake, a curved pipe of bamboo, at the end of which the mouth-piece is fitted. The bottoms, or water vessels, are made of composition, but smaller than the *Hookah* bottoms, and more of an urn shape in general. The smoker usually holds the *Goorgoory* in his hand. The lower classes of natives all smoke the *Goorgoory*, made of a cocoa nut, with only a straight bamboo pipe, serving as a snake, and without any mouth-piece. This apparatus, indeed, is an indispensable part of the travelling baggage of even the poorest among them: and to such a pitch is their passion for smoking carried, that it is common to see a *Goorgoory* slung to some part of a gentleman's palankeen, when he is going but a few miles from home. When resting, or waiting for their master, the bearers obtain some lighted charcoal, and soon put the *Goorgoory* in motion, passing it round in high style, and playing at patcheess, on the ground; where, by means of pieces of brick, stones, &c. they continue to get through many a well-contested game; though the checkers, which form the tables, be only scratched on the soil, by means of a stick, or other implement.

The natives of opulence always retain in their *harams*, or seraglios, some women, who are skilful in preparing tobacco; and are, in all respects, capable of furnishing the *Goorgoory* in perfect order. Such are easily to be found in a country, where smoking is as common as beer-drinking is with us. However, some are more gifted than others with the talent of making up tobacco; and of placing it on the *towah*, or tile; which, however simple it may appear, is an operation requiring some judgment. Fragrant tobacco is not always to be had; nor can it always be distinguished, on account of the general practice of pouring rose water into the snake.

Those who keep dancing girls, provide also female musicians, or eunuchs; no male attendants being admitted within the *zenonah*. An apartment is selected in the coolest part of the interior, where a light bedding being spread on carpets, the great man lolls at his ease; being furnished with various small pillows, and having one very large bolster at the part next the wall. Being sewed with his *Hookah*, or *Goorgoory*, as he may prefer; and having all the apparatus for beetle, which he chews incessantly, at his side; not forgetting a *peek-daun*, or spitting-pot, the idle gentleman passes hour after hour, and day after day, in the same dull, effeminate, and ignorant course.

The music generally consists of one or more *sarindahs*, or fiddles, played as they are rested on the knee; a pair of small cymbals, shaped like bells; a *tom-tom*, or long drum; and a pair of *tablahs*, or very small kettle drums; which, as well as the *tom-tom*, are beat with the fingers only. Much skill is displayed on these rude materials; which, however they may be tolerated as a novelty, never fail to weary those unlucky auditors, who often are compelled, rather than give offence, to have their heads stunned, and their nerves disordered, by the monotonous and shrill notes which, for hours together, vibrate on their wearied ears. Such is the *music* of the East!

# PLATE XX.

## MARQUIS WELLESLEY AND HIS SUITE, AT THE NABOB OF OUDE'S BREAKFAST TABLE, VIEWING AN ELEPHANT-FIGHT.

THE mention of two elephants contending, naturally raises ideas of the most sanguine nature, and excites our curiosity to behold a combat, which, from the bulk and powers of the animals engaged, we pre-suppose must be replete with interest. In this, however, the spectator is grievously disappointed; for, except that the instigated beasts now and then press against each other's heads, and clash their teeth, there appears little effort, and much less of skill, in either party. Sometimes, indeed, one of the elephants will run off, in which case the other follows for a short distance, but soon relapses into his wonted placidity. The late Nabob of Lucknow, *Asoph al Dowlah*, whose intellects were as heavy as his enormous head, derived much pleasure from such spectacles; and often expressed his surprise, that our Governor-General did not amuse himself and his court in a similar manner. He might have learnt, from experience, that the British government was intent on contests of much greater importance!

XX.

London, Published & Sold by Edwd. Orme. March 1st 1813.

The nabobs and sonbahs, throughout India, are in the habit of giving public breakfasts, and of occasionally inviting all the European gentlemen, in their vicinity, to grand dinners, *nautches*, or dances, and other amusements. On such occasions, a profusion of viands, dressed both in the European and Hindostanee modes, are served up; the greatest variety is seen, with the exception of swine's flesh, which, being interdicted by the *Koran*, or Mahometan Book of Faith, could not be tolerated. However, many very *excellent* Mussulmans, who are above prejudice, and whose situations place them beyond the reach of their ecclesiastic law, are often seen, when among Europeans, and in the absence of the servants, to eat substantial slices of ham, under the designation of *Belatty Herron*, or English venison, for which they pretend to receive it. Wine is equally prohibited by the *Koran*, but is now drank without reserve by many of the principal natives; though, in general, they either pretend not to know what it is, or to take it medicinally. In fact, the bigots of India are now materially softening down the rigours of their religion.

The Plate exhibits the open *verandah*, or balcony, of the Nabob's palace, at Lucknow, where the breakfast table is laid. It is situated on the bank of the *Goomty*, or winding river, so denominated from its irregular course, which meanders in such a manner, as to cause the distance, from Lucknow to Benares, to be three times as great by water as it is by land. The *Goomty* is in few places more than two hundred yards over: in the rainy season, it runs with wondrous impetuosity. The elephant fight is represented on the opposite bank.

# A Brief History

OF

# ANCIENT AND MODERN INDIA,

BY

F. W. BLAGDON, ESQ.

# ADDRESS.

WITHOUT some definite and reasonable apology, the man who should attempt to write a History of the most celebrated country in the world, in so short a compass as the following, would be liable not merely to censure, but perhaps to ridicule. However, the Author confidently hopes, that Brief as is the space to which he has been confined, the Sketch will be entitled to consideration; not merely as a compilement from voluminous writers (for he has brought it down to the present time from authentic sources of information, resulting from his private connexions), but as a chronological arrangement of the events that have transpired in a great portion of the eastern quarter of the world, collected from documents various, authentic, and extensive; events which, from their nature and consequences, particularly in modern times, can be considered with no common satisfaction by every admirer of British generosity, mildness, and valour. It will enable the Reader, who may be unacquainted with Asiatic affairs, to form a correct idea of the immense and interesting territory which has so often been the scite of British bravery, and which will doubtless long prove a primary source of British opulence.

But in order that the nature of this literary addition may be more completely understood, it should be observed, that brevity was throughout indispensably necessary, being originally written to accompany a collection of large folio engravings, Views in India; and the rapid pressure of important events having left no place for those reflections and remarks which must always arise from historical composition, the Sketch should rather be considered as a narrative of the most striking occurrences; and in which those of our own age have been discussed more in detail than those of remote periods, of which little is known with certainty, but which are supposed chiefly to have had their origin in hypothetical report. Hence, the Author, from a presentiment of their superior importance, has confined his account to the political, military, and commercial incidents of the general history; and has found no room for the introduction of the religious dogmata and civil regulations, which prevail in such complex and varied shades, throughout the territory of India. Such an omission will, he trusts, be the more excusable, from the difficulty, the impossibility, of conveying in a satisfactory manner, and in a contracted space, the veriest outline of the abstruse systems of Hindoo theology, and Hindoo laws.

A

# BRIEF HISTORY,

*&c. &c.*

FROM the earliest periods of antiquity, that extensive portion of Asia denominated Hind, Hindostan, or India, has been eminently distinguished, not only by its favourable climate and the striking peculiarity of its productions, in which the majesty and simplicity of nature are, in a high degree, conspicuous; but particularly by the various temporal changes and revolutions to which it has been subjected. Equally wonderful and admirable is the moral and religious character of its inhabitants, whether we regard their systematic division into various tribes, their rigid adherence to the different shades of worship professed by their forefathers, their placid and submissive disposition, their general inclination to temperance, or their great ingenuity in all the mechanical professions. Indeed, in whatever view the ancient and modern history of this empire is considered, it cannot fail to afford a more diversified and awful subject for contemplation, than is to be derived from that of any other country in the habitable world.

Although it is to be regretted, that in the ancient history of every nation truth is manifestly blended with fiction, and that all the accounts transmitted previous to the commencement of written history are vague and unsatisfactory, yet we have authority too great to be doubted, that the mild and fertile regions of the East formed the residence of man, when placed on earth by the Creator to begin his career of mortality; and, by minute comparison it has appeared, that a very considerable analogy exists between the account of the creation, deluge, &c. contained in the Puranas, or sacred writings of the Hindoos, and that which forms the substance of the book of Genesis. Independently, therefore, of its interest as an extensive record of the most celebrated empire in the world, the ancient account of India becomes particularly important, from its similitude with the sacred volumes transmitted to us by the inspired writers; while its modern history must be peculiarly interesting, as it exhibits the importance of the British possessions, acquired by a series of valourous actions, not surpassed by any of which our countrymen have to boast. But as moral and political reflections on this subject, however frequent the opportunities for them may occur, can neither be given nor expected in a historical account which, from its contracted limits, must be considered only as an outline of important facts, we shall proceed at once to our narrative; merely premising, that no authority, however extensive, has been overlooked, nor have any exertions been omitted, which could render, in this Sketch, a faithful abstract of the great events recorded by voluminous writers on the Indian history.

The ancient empire of India extended from the vast chain of mountains of Thebet and Tartary in the North, to the island of Ceylon on the South; and from the great river Ganges on the East, to that of Indus on the West. These rivers are at a distance of four hundred leagues from each other: the whole extent of territory contains as many square miles as are comprised in about half the continent of Europe; and the amount of its population is by some writers computed at nearly sixty-five, by others at seventy millions. It was called by the ancient inhabitants *Bharat Varsa*, and comprehended all those countries in which the primitive religion and laws of Brahma were predominant.

The two grand and principal rivers, after diffusing the most luxuriant verdure through many rich and powerful kingdoms in their passage, fall into the Ocean; the one by various mouths in the 24th degree of west latitude, comprising the country of Kartsh; the other into the Bay of Bengal, between Chittagong and Diamond Point, in the 22d degree of east latitude; while on three sides the country is bounded by vast ridges of stupendous mountains, one of which extends from north to south, completely across the territory, which thus possesses the most pleasing variety of climate; and, at its opposite extremities, exhibits the singular phenomenon of two seasons at the same period. If we also consider the immense natural treasures of this region, such as the abundance of its agricultural products, its valuable aromatic woods, its delicious fruits, and the richness and variety of its manufactures, the vast object of contemplation will be increased; but we shall have no cause for surprise, that such a wonderful country has always afforded a field for the ambition and rapacity of military conquerors.

That part of the empire denominated Hindostan, is comprised between the latitude of 21 and 30 degrees north, and signifies *the country of the black people.* By the *Deccan*, which implies south, is understood the great Indian peninsula; and the word India was used by the Greeks, according to Strabo, Arrian, Ptolemy, and others, to define the immense territory that lies between Persia and China, the mountains of Tartary, and the Southern Ocean; but, in Europe, we now understand by Hindostan, or India, the whole of those extensive countries comprised within all the above-mentioned limits, including Ceylon and the different islands in the Eastern Archipelago. The term India is therefore very considerable in its application, though it more properly relates only to the ancient empire of Hindostan. The remote antiquity of the nations of this empire has often given rise to the most attractive theories of philosophers; but, it must be admitted, that their opinions have hitherto only rested on conjecture; and, as history is a branch of literature which has never been cultivated by the Hindoos, nothing can be expected like a regular narration of the events which have taken place in their country during the early ages. The general opinion, however, is, that the Hindoos, as they appear at present, were the aboriginal inhabitants of the territory in question; and this idea is strongly supported by Mr. Orme, the historian, who observes, that "they have no relation in their figures and manners to any of the contiguous nations." A striking argument in support of this opinion may also be drawn from the permanency of their religious system; which, though resting on the fragile bases of idolatry and superstition, has, according to the most authentic accounts, remained unaltered through successive generations, for a period of 3000 years.

The earliest description of these extraordinary people was written by Megasthenes; who, about 2000 years ago, was sent as ambassador from Seleucus, the Grecian emperor, to Sandracottos, king of Prachi, the ancient name for the provinces of Bengal, Bahar, and a part of Oude;* and, it is very remarkable, that his account fully corresponds with every material part of their modern history. One circumstance, however, which has undoubtedly tended to preserve the purity of their origin, is that part of their religious ordinances, which prohibits them from intermarrying with foreigners; and which would be considered as entailing perpetual infamy upon themselves and their posterity.

As the Hindoos were ever a pacific people, though celebrated for their courage and perseverance, they did not cultivate the art of war; and their necessary military establishments not being systematically conducted, their early victories are attributable rather to their valour and perseverance than to their scientific ingenuity. The losses which they sustained in combating with their more experienced enemies were supplied by hordes of slaves, whom their

* He resided a long time at Baliputra, and his journals having fallen into the possession of Arrian, they were incorporated by him in his history of India. This history is often quoted by the ancients; but Lempriere, in his "Bibliotheca," asserts, that what now passes as his composition is spurious.

laws authorized them to purchase, or enfranchise among themselves, and who were taken from all classes promiscuously, except the Brahmuns. These slaves were not only compelled to undertake military duties, but were considered as a part of the establishment of all persons of consequence, whose importance seemed to be proportionate to the number they were capable of supporting:—those however employed about the household of the great men were principally prisoners of war, who were doomed to such degrading servitude, as the consequence of their captivity; but those employed as auxiliaries in the battles, derived such aid from their ingenuity and perseverance, that they were often enabled to diffuse terror amongst the firm and disciplined warriors of Greece. For many centuries previous to the invasion of Alexander, they had become acquainted with gunpowder and fire-arms; and, at the time of this invasion, the Macedonian armies, on the banks of the Hyphasis, were disconcerted and appalled, by the artillery of wood and iron, with which the Hindoos defended their walls, and by the rockets which they threw in amongst them; the effect of which was attributed by the assailants to supernatural agency.

As ancient India was celebrated from the earliest times for its wisdom and its wealth, it was natural that the envy, cupidity, and hatred of neighbouring and even distant countries should be excited against it. The transmission of its luxuries to the fairs of Babylon and Tyre, and their conveyance into Egypt and Greece by the Phœnicians, who opened the navigation between the Red Sea and the coasts of Malabar and Guzerat, first gave rise to the opinion, that by a general, or even partial conquest of the country, they might be procured on easier terms; and thus we ascertain the primeval cause of those numerous and sanguinary battles, massacres, and invasions, from which this famous empire has derived a vast portion of its celebrity.

It is stated in the Puranas, that Hindostan was, for many centuries, divided into various kingdoms; which, though independent of each other, nevertheless acknowledged one sovereign, more potent than the rest, as their supreme head, and with whom they all united to repel any aggression of foreign nations. Previous to the invasion of Alexander, the empire is reported to have comprised four powerful kingdoms, viz.

1. Prachi, or the East, including Bengal, Bahar, and a part of Oude, and of which the metropolis was Baliputra, so celebrated in Grecian history by the name of Palibothra.*

2. The kingdom which comprehended the great peninsula from the river Kistnah to Cape Comorin, and which was afterwards celebrated for the splendour of its metropolis of Bijanagur, said to have been founded in the third century of the Hegira.

3. The kingdom which extended from the Gulph of Cambay to the mouths of the Ganges; and from latitude 22 to 17 degrees north; comprising the provinces of Guzerat, Malwa, Candeish, Berar, and Dowlatabad, according to the map of Major Rennell.

4. The kingdom which comprised the provinces of Lahore, Multan, Delhi, and Ajimeer, and which were governed by Rajahs,

* Vide Mr. Wilford's Treatise on Hindoo Chronology, Asiatic Researches. Vol. V.

or petty princes, who were tributary and responsible to their respective sovereigns.

The northern states of India having formed a confederacy, which was influenced by the same laws and superstitions, but which differed essentially in language, manners, and interests, a basis was thus laid for frequent dissentions, which attracted the attention of the Persians, and barbarian Tartars of Thebet, and caused their irruptions into those wealthy provinces. One good effect, however, resulted from this connexion; for it enabled the princes of the West to make an astonishing resistance to the conquering phalanxes of Alexander, though their patriotic efforts were ultimately ineffectual, as the discipline and martial skill of the Greeks finally bore down all before them; and Alexander, after having subdued several states on the banks of the Indus, passed the rivers of the Panjab, attacked the powerful army collected by the valiant prince Porus, to oppose his progress; when, though he had to encounter a most gallant resistance, he obtained a decisive victory by the capture of the prince and his most distinguished generals. His brilliant career, however, was of short duration; as a mutiny, which soon afterwards broke out in his camp, obliged him to make a precipitate retreat from Hindostan, leaving the conquered territory in possession of a few of his officers, with a small part of his army:—but the wealth, honours, and luxurious habits, which they had acquired, too soon abolished those feelings which support the dignity of the soldier; and a succession of vice and debauchery, to which the oppressed Hindoos did not fail to administer, caused the rapid destruction of the Macedonian victors. This event was indeed facilitated by the death of Alexander, which happened about the time alluded to, or 330 years before Christ, and by the subsequent division of his empire; while the remains of his power in Hindostan were finally reduced by the valourous conduct of Chandra-gupta, king of Prachi. This prince was the son of Nanda, whose character for wisdom and bravery is always described in terms of admiration by the Hindoos, and who was murdered by a faithless domestic, in revenge for some imaginary injury. He left several sons, who disputed the succession with the utmost rancour; but the majority of the nobles being in favour of Chandra-gupta, he took possession of the throne, after a sanguinary conflict with his contentious brothers.

Several of the western Powers afforded this prince material assistance in support of his claims, by the contribution of their own, as well as of Greek soldiers, whom they had bribed into their service; and soon after, the Grecian prince Seleucus, having advanced towards the Indus, with intent to recover the possessions obtained by Alexander, the king of Prachi previously entered those territories; and, after restoring them to the powers from whom they had been wrested, he offered battle to Seleucus, which the latter thought proper to decline, notwithstanding the brows of his troops were crowned with the laurels of recent victories. On the contrary, he even made proposals of peace, which were accepted by Chandra-gupta, and by which the Greeks abandoned all pretensions to the conquests of Alexander on the east bank of the Indus: the king of Prachi, who was only actuated by motives of patriotism and justice, then returned to his capital amidst the admiration of his subjects. But Seleucus had wisely secured to the Greeks the most extensive commercial advantages, and by his apparent candour, had obtained the good opinion of Chandra-gupta; so that the latter consented to receive the celebrated Megasthenes at the court of Baliputra, where he resided several years, and succeeded in restoring the trade which had formerly existed between the two countries.

At length, after raising his empire to a degree of unparallelled prosperity, Chandra-gupta closed a glorious reign; and his successors are said to have pursued the same system of patriotic benevolence; but his family became extinct about 200 years before Christ; and from that period till the invasion of the Mahomedans, the history of Hindostan is buried in obscurity; though the poets have recorded innumerable anecdotes of commotions and civil wars, which may, in part at least, be supposed to have foundation in truth. We are informed, by them that the Bactrians, having revolted from the Seleucidæ, or descendants of Seleucus, in the decline of the Assyrian power, the inhabitants of the small states, which had been subdued by Alexander, frequently united to repel the aggressions of the first-mentioned people, and the brave resistance which they made, rendered them worthy of a fate far different from that to which they ultimately submitted.

It was in the seventh century of the Christian æra, doubtless the most important in the Indian history, that the Arabs, in consequence of their predilection for traffic, and their ardour for conversion to the Mahomedan faith, became anxious for the most daring enterprizes; and, under the pretence of commercial dealings, they crossed the Indian Ocean to Guzerat, Malabar, and all the southern parts of India, where they insiduously disseminated their new religion, while in the Northern Provinces they were endeavouring to enforce it by the sword. Hence it appears, that by the 10th century of the Christian æra, or the fourth of the Hegira, they had converted the inhabitants of Korasan and Kabul, and established in those provinces the kingdom of Ghizni. They had also crossed the Indus, pillaged all the Hindoo temples in Lahore, and returned to Ghizni with the spoils, when Mahmoud I. upon his accession to the throne of Ghizni, made the impious vow to convert, by force of arms, the whole Hindoo race to the Mahomedan faith. He immediately began with the most horrid cruelties, spared neither age nor sex; and, in the course of twenty years, he had twelve times invaded Hindostan, and conquered the whole of the western provinces, from Guzerat to Delhi. The princes of Guzerat, indeed, made a brave resistance; but, being finally subdued, the whole of the population, who could not effect their escape, were put to the sword with the most sanguinary triumph.

The plunder of the conquered provinces having made Mahmoud the most wealthy monarch of his race, he at length quitted Hindostan; and, after residing some time in his native country, turned his arms against the Persians and Tartars, in whose immense regions his victories were equally rapid, cruel, and astonishing.

After the death of Mahmoud, which happened A.D. 1030, the same system of persecution was continued by his successors, and several attempts were made by the native princes to avenge their injuries, but particularly by the prince of Delhi, who having raised a powerful army, defeated the Mussulmans in several general engagements; but, elated with his success, he continued the pursuit with too great impetuosity; and, in the year 1046, after a dreadful conflict, his whole army was completely defeated.

From this period nothing important is known till 1191, when Mahomed Ghori, an Afghan prince, conquered Ghizni; and, penetrating into the eastern provinces, fought many severe battles with the Hindoo princes, whom he finally overcame, ravaged the provinces of Oude and Allahabad, stormed the city of Benares; and, after devoting that ancient seat of literature and science to general pillage, he consecrated the temple of Brahma to the prophet of Mecca, and invoked his spirit to sanction the abominable outrage. But an insurrection having broken out at Korasan, he was obliged to leave Benares to subdue the insurgents: here, however, his fortune changed; for the prince of Samarcand having arrived with a powerful reinforcement for the Korasanians, Mahomed, after a most desperate defence, was driven into a small fort, and surrounded by the enemy; from whom he ransomed himself for a large sum of money, and returned to Ghizni, where he was assassinated, after a powerful reign of thirty years.

On the death of this chief, the empire of Ghizni was usurped by Eldoze and Cuttubeddin, who had been the confidential officers of Mahmoud; the former took possession of Turkestan and Persia; while the latter, who was originally a slave in the country of the

Afghans, declared himself king of Hindostan, and founded the Afghan Dynasty. He then formed a plan for, and partially succeeded in, conquering Bahar and Bengal; but his premature death left his projects of usurpation to be completed by Altemesh, who ascended the throne of Delhi in A. D. 1210, and whose dominions in 1225 extended from the mountains of Thebet to the Deccan, in latitude 20 degrees north, and from the Ganges to t e Indus. He was an enlightened prince; but the oppressions of those, whom he had appointed as governors, always kept the inhabitants of the western provinces in a state of revolt, and often led to sanguinary conflicts.

In 1231, the celebrated Zinghis Khan conquered all Asia to the northward of latitude 30 degrees, as well as all the countries on the west bank of the Indus, which he distributed amongst his Mogul chieftains. These afterwards made many incursions into the Panjab, and to the borders of Delhi, where they were at length defeated by the virtuous Balin, who succeeded Altemesh; and by whose noble and magnanimous conduct, the empire was restored to a degree of quiet and prosperity which it had not enjoyed for centuries This monarch died in 1286, and was succeeded by Kei-Kobad and Ferose the Second, in whose reigns nothing particular occurred; but the usurper Alla, having ascended the throne of Hindostan in 1306, by the murder of his uncle Ferose, the Mussulman power was extended over the northern provinces of the Deccan. Alla appears to have been one of the most detestable tyrants in the history of that country. He resorted to every kind of profligacy and oppression, in order to gain the ends of his ambition. He seized the property of all men of wealth, forbade the nobles to marry without obtaining his license, and declared that religion had no connexion with civil government; while in those provinces, where the largesses could not be furnished, he pillaged all the sacred temples with unrelenting rapacity.

During these proceedings in the Deccan, the Moguls besieged Delhi with a powerful army; but Alla, suddenly returning to the defence of his capital, totally defeated the assailants, after one of the most sanguinary battles recorded in Indian history. This event did not fail to increase the pride, and stimulate the ambition of the chieftain, whose future schemes of conquest were extraordinary and eccentric. He was not contented with gaining the title of a great commander, but was anxious to be considered as a prophet; and, by laying the foundation of a new religion, to excel in power and in fame both Alexander and Mahomed. But though Alla possessed a comprehensive mind, he was greatly deficient in many qualities, which would have been necessary to the success of a project of far less magnitude than that which his vanity had suggested; and he soon saw an insurmountable obstacle to the execution of his schemes, in the disaffection of his nobility; while he became convinced of the danger of innovation upon the doctrines of the Hindoos, whose adherents had ever supported them with the mildest, though most decisive firmness. At length he was forced to abandon his unlimited projects, and to amuse himself with the prospect of conquering the southern countries of Hindostan. But even here his ambition was for a long time frustrated; for the irruptions of the Moguls into his northern provinces, kept him in continual warfare, in order to secure the possessions he had already acquired; while his own presence was necessary at the head of the forces which were to repel the invaders. He however dispatched Cafoor, one of his most experienced generals, against the Hindoo kingdoms to the north of the Kistnah; all of which, except the mountainous tracts of Orissa and Berar, were conquered by this commander, who returned to Delhi with plunder from the Deccan, which amounted to one hundred millions sterling.

Alla being now satiated with hostility, endeavoured to pass his life in peace, and nothing worthy of notice occurred during the remainder of his reign. He made many judicious and systematic arrangements in the administration of public affairs throughout his immense dominions, which he had increased by upwards of half of the peninsula of India; and, notwithstanding his sanguinary and despotic conduct at the commencement of his power, he died respected by his subjects; who, reflecting only on the advantages which they then enjoyed, forgot the outrages by which he had become their master.

After the death of Alla, however, his system of government was abandoned by his puerile successors, and anarchy soon prevailed throughout the empire; when, by the exertions of the Hindoo princes, who always cautiously watched for an opportunity of avenging themselves upon their oppressors, a powerful confederacy was formed in the Deccan, and the whole of the Peninsula, except the fortress of Dowlatabad and part of Candeish, was taken from the Mussulmans by Balaldeo, king of the Carnatic. They were also assailed from the north by the descendants of Zinghis Khan, who saw in their wealth an incessant stimulus to conquest. Thus, in the minority of Mahmoud III. the Mussulman empire, in India, was not only attacked by the Hindoos in the south, and the Moguls in the north, but was disturbed, for three years, by the most furious intestine divisions; during the whole of which period, the city of Delhi was scarcely ever free from sanguinary conflicts between the adherents of the rival potentates; till, at length, both parties being nearly exhausted, they agreed upon a truce, in order amicably to settle their differences.

It was during this suspension of hostilities that the invasion of the famous Timur Bec, or Tamerlane, formed one of the most important æras in the history of India. This prince, who was the chief of the Muguls, the king of Candahar, and the lineal descendant of Zinghis Khan, having subdued all the northern nations of Asia, and extended his conquests as far as the eastern provinces of Russia, formed the project of subjugating Hindostan; and accordingly proceeded with an immense army from Samarcand to the Jallali, a western branch of the Indus, and thence down the river to the confluence of the Jimboo and the Chinab, where he passed over his army on a bridge of boats; and, meeting with resistance from the populous town of Tulmubini, he plundered the inhabitants of their property, and put them all to the sword. This event happened about the close of the year 1398.

The terrific proceedings of this new conqueror, who had spread desolation through the whole province of Multan, caused an union between the factions at Delhi, whence, on his approach, the sultan Mahmoud and his minister Eckbal sallied out against him; but after a conflict of several hours, they were repulsed with considerable loss. It is asserted, that some of the prisoners taken by Timur's army, having expressed their exultation at the bravery of their countrymen, he barbarously ordered the whole of the victims in his possession to be massacred; and, according to Ferishta, "upwards of 100,000 of these people were, in less than an hour, put to the sword!" On the following day a general assault was made by Timur, which was encountered by a sortie on the part of Eckbal; but being again defeated with great slaughter, he advised Mahmoud to retreat to Guzerat, whither he was pursued by a detachment from Timur, and only effected his escape after the loss of two of his sons, and a considerable part of his retinue.

In the mean time the conqueror entered Delhi, and levied contributions in proportion to the wealth of the inhabitants; but, on some resistance taking place, he gave orders for a general massacre, which was carried into effect, and the city literally deluged with the blood of its inhabitants. He also, at a grand festival to commemorate his victories, caused another general sacrifice of all the prisoners in his possession, not excepting women and children.—In short, nothing could satiate his enmity towards the Hindoos; and, marching to the rocks of Coupele, which form a sacred cave at the foot of

Mount Kimmaleh, he is said to have put to death several thousand pilgrims in the act of their devotion.

At length the incursions of sultan Bajazet in the north of Asia caused Timur to repair to Samarcand; and, having left no force to keep possession of his conquests in Hindostan, they became again the prey of civil commotions, which ended in the restoration of Mahmoud to his throne, which he retained till his death in A.D. 1413; but his power was merely nominal, the provinces having been deprived of all their wealth and grandeur, by the victorious and inexorable marauders by whom they had been ravaged.

The throne of Delhi was next occupied by a family of Seids, or, as they called themselves, descendants of the holy prophet; but their feeble dynasty terminated in 1450, by the abdication of Alla, their last prince, and the elevation of Belloli, of Affghan, who reigned 38 years; when, in 1488, the empire was again dismembered: but the influence of Belloli only extended through the province of Delhi, a Mussulman having usurped the title of king of Bengal and Bahar; while in the Deccan, to the north of the Kistnah, there were five independent Mussulman states.

The power of the monarchs of Delhi was however for some time transitory; Secunder, the son of Belloli, having reigned with some *éclat* till 1509, and transferred the seat of government to Agra: but, under Ibrahim, son of the latter, the people became rebellious; and, uniting with sultan Baber, a Mogul prince, he was totally defeated, and expired in the field of battle. The sultan, who had literally descended from Timur, then took possession of Delhi and Agra, caused himself to be proclaimed emperor; and thus, in 1525, began a new Mogul dynasty, after making, with this object in view, four different irruptions into Hindostan. He was an amiable prince, and was alike celebrated for his heroism and his generosity; but he existed only five years after the conquest of Delhi:—he tolerated religion, and was celebrated for his skill in poetry and music.

Humaioon, his son, was a prince whose career was equally victorious. He subjugated the western provinces of Guzerat and Malwa, and those of Bengal and Bahar on the east; but, being attacked by the united force of his younger brothers, he was obliged to abandon Hindostan, and retire to Persia. The brothers afterwards quarelled, and were subdued by Shere, an Affghan prince, who was proclaimed emperor in 1542; but, after nine years of exile, Humaioon returned to Hindostan at the head of a considerable Persian army; and, defeating the Affghans at Sirhind, regained his title and power. His son Akbar, though only 13 years of age at the time of this victory, displayed the greatest military genius; and, succeeding his father in 1556, the country enjoyed under him a succession of uninterrupted prosperity.* At his death, in 1605, the Mussulman princes again attacked the remaining dependencies of the Hindoo monarchy of Bejanaghur, which comprised the whole of

* A full account of the life and character of this monarch is to be found in the "*Ayeen Akbery*," or the Institutes of the Emperor Akbar, translated by Francis Gladwin, Esq.—This learned potentate is particularly alluded to in those excellent works, the "Asiatic Researches" and the "Asiatic Annual Register."

the peninsula from the river Kistnah to Cape Comorin, and had never been subdued till 1565, when Ram Ramjee, the Hindoo king, was defeated and killed by the Mahomedans at the battle of Tellecottah; but the southern provinces of this kingdom, Mysore, Bidenore, Ginjee, Tritchinopoly, Tanjore, and Madura, had remained independent, under naicks, or governors, after the dissolution of the kingdom of Bejanaghur: and, in consequence of the conquest abovementioned, the Malabar states of Cochin, Travancore, Calicut, &c. also shook off their dependency.

When the Mussulman princes of the Deccan approached, after the death of Akbar, towards these states, they met with little or no opposition; as the people of this part of the country had become accustomed to the manners of the Mahomedans, by the intercourse of the Turkish merchants amongst them, and had no apprehension of conquest, but rather wished for their arrival, to assist in the expulsion of the Portugueze, who had at this time become a fierce and troublesome body of invaders.—It was at this period, also, that the British flag was first displayed triumphant on the coasts of India.

For many centuries the general commerce with India, notwithstanding the commotions with which that country was always afflicted, had attained the most extensive success. It was first raised to a degree of unexampled eminence under the auspicious influence of the Romans, who proceeded by sea from the straits of Babelmandel to Guzerat and Malabar: this route was discovered by Hippalus, a naval captain in the time of Augustus; and from that period till the decline of the Roman empire, a fleet of 120 ships annually sailed from Myos-hormos, in the Red Sea, to Musiris and Borace, now called Meerjee and Barcelore, on the coast of Malabar. The profits of this extensive commerce appear to have been greatly in favour of India, as the Romans gave specie in exchange for all their articles of luxury; and this circumstance, added to the propensity of the Hindoos for hoarding their money, together with their own natural resources, may account for the great wealth with which that country in early times abounded. On the decline of the Roman Empire, at the period when the government was removed to Constantinople, their commerce with India was likewise depreciated; but this decrease is supposed to have originated, not from the declension of the European power, but from the excessive opulence and consequent idleness of the merchants of Alexandria, through whose medium it was carried on by way of the Red Sea. The spirit of commercial enterprise, however, as it declined amongst the Egyptians, was seized by the Arabs, who, stimulated by the ardour of propagating the Mahomedan religion, as well as by a thirst for plunder, under the name of traffic, equipped annually several squadrons of ships for Malabar, and obtained leave to settle as merchants at the sea-ports.

When we consider the mild and acquiescent manners of the Hindoos, to which those of the Arabs were not dissimilar, it will not appear surprising that the latter soon obtained a permanent footing amongst the natives: hence we learn that in A.D. 642, or the 21st of the Hegira, they built a mosque at Corrigalore, as well as several others on different parts of the coast; where, notwithstanding the opposition they experienced from the Jewish and other Christian merchants, they succeeded in making thousands of converts to their faith; most of whom, however, were either Brahminical outcasts, or those who escaped from the persecutions of their governors and petty tyrants in the north of India. To the abovementioned cause (the passive disposition of the Hindoos) is also to be attributed the diffusion of every other worship known in civilized nations, and nearly all of which have existed in India since the commencement of the ninth century of the Christian æra. We know from undisputed authority, that Christianity was introduced into India by the apostles, particularly by St. Thomas and St. Panthene; and it is asserted, that the latter, on his arrival, found amongst the natives, a copy of the Gospel of St. Matthew in Hebrew:—the first appearance of this religion, therefore, in India, must have taken place in the first and second ages of the church. It cannot, however, be expected, that we should be able to enter much into the ecclesiastical history of India; and, having merely noticed the origin of the different systems in that country, we shall proceed to the continuation of the political and commercial incidents, which it is our object to record.

When the spirit of traffic declined amongst the Egyptians, it was not only assumed by the Arabs, but likewise by the Persians, who sent ships to Malabar and Ceylon, which returned with the commodities of India and China to the Euphrates and the Tigris, whence they were conveyed to Assyria, and finally to Constantinople: and this commercial preponderance of the Persians continued to increase till the end of the sixth century, by which time they had monopolized nearly the whole trade of Asia:—it however declined with them after the conquest of Syria and Egypt by the Caliph Amrou; who, in the year 639, prohibited the merchants of Alexandria from their usual intercourse with the Byzantine empire. But during two centuries from this period, it was revived by some adventurous merchants of Constantinople; who, procuring the productions of Amol and Urkanje, two towns on the west bank of the Oxus, carried them thence down that river to the Caspian Sea.

Thus the commerce of India was divided between the empires of Persia and Byzantium, till the 10th century, when the spirit of enterprise again seized the then degenerate inhabitants of Greece and Italy; and the Eastern trade having thus been revived by these merchants, its produce was soon diffused through most of the countries of Europe. A more considerable extent was, however, given to this traffic by the crusades, which greatly facilitated the intercourse between Europe and India; and it was still further promoted by the partition of the Grecian Empire, in the year 1104, when the Venetians, having obtained a part of the Morea, and some islands in the Archipelago, they became the rivals of the Italians in Eastern commerce. They were, however, soon discomfited by the Genoese, who formed a confederacy with some schismatic Greeks, and deprived the Venetians of the inland trade to China: but the latter having succeeded in obtaining a bull from the Pope, to carry on a free trade with infidels, they again recovered their influence; and, by residing in the commercial towns of Egypt, they continued a flourishing traffic with India, by way of the Red Sea and the Persian Gulf; while the Genoese carried on the northern trade between India and Constantinople.

In this state did the Indian commerce continue till the expulsion of the Genoese from the Byzantine Empire, at its conquest in 1453 by Mahomed II. who established the Turkish power in Europe. By this revolution, it fell entirely into the possession of the Venetians in Egypt, with whom it continued till the important discovery was made by the Portugueze, of the passage to India round the southern extremity of Africa. The enterprises of these people were commenced under the government of Don Henry, count de Viseo, in the year 1420; and, encouraged by the discovery of Madeira, Porto Santo, and other islands, they were continued by Diaz and Vasquez de Gama, the latter of whom passed the Cape of Good Hope on the 20th of November, 1497, and arrived safely at Mozambique, where he was assailed both by disease and fanaticism; his men being attacked by the scurvy, while the Mahomedans were seeking every means to destroy them, as soon as they knew that they were Christians. The prudence and care, however, of de Gama, overcame all these difficulties, and he proceeded from Mozambique to Melinda, where the prince gave him a gracious reception: from hence he pursued his course east, across the great Indian Ocean; and, on the 22d of May, 1498, he reached Calicut, on the coast of Malabar. Here he was received hospitably by the Zamorin, who granted the Portugueze permission to trade, provided they did not molest the Mahomedans, and other nations who enjoyed the same advantages; after which he returned to Portugal, and obtained the highest honours and rewards for his services.

The unexpected success of this enterprise excited a degree of emulation amongst the different nations of Europe; while, on the other hand, the Portugueze, elated with their prosperity, conceived that nothing could be more easy than to monopolize the whole trade of India with Europe, and with this view, an extensive force was sent out, under Don Pedro de Capral, to form an establishment at Malabar. In this expedition the fleet consisted of about 30 sail, including several ships of the line; and, amongst other appendages of the equipment, a number of priests were sent out, for the purpose of converting the Hindoos and Mahomedans to the Catholic religion. Capral sailed from Lisbon in March, 1500; and, on his passage, he discovered, by steering westward, the important country of Brazil, or the east part of South America, of which he took possession, by establishing the flag of Portugal, and denominating it the "Land of the Holy Cross." He then pursued his voyage, and arrived at Calicut, after losing five of his ships, when he was received in the most friendly manner by the Zamorin, who allowed him to open factories, and plant the flag of Portugal in his dominions. But the haughty disposition of this commander, and the misconduct of his people, involved him in continual broils with the natives, and at length caused the Zamorin to take part against him; on which he joined the rajah of Cochin, who was at war with the lastmentioned potentate. Here, however, the same supercilious conduct soon causing him to be despised, and his offers being rejected by the princes of Malabar, he was obliged to return to Lisbon, without any other advantage than that of having contrived to load his ships with a valuable cargo.

The Portugueze, however, were not to be deterred by a partial failure, from attempting to realize their splendid speculations; and Emanuel, as if anticipating the events which would result from the haughty behaviour of Capral, had, even in the interim, dispatched a small squadron under the orders of Don Juan Nova Colleca, who, learning of the differences which had arisen between the Zamorin and Capral, first sailed for Cannanore, and thence to Cochin. On his way to the lastmentioned place, he fell in with a fleet of vessels belonging to the Zamorin, which he almost totally destroyed. The rajah of Cochin received him in the most friendly manner; and, returning shortly to Europe with a valuable cargo, he discovered and took possession of the important island of St. Helena. In the mean time the Portugueze government fitted out another large fleet, which sailed from Lisbon for Cannanore in the beginning of 1503, under the command of Vasquez de Gama, who was then at a very advanced age. It arrived in safety, and acquired a most valuable cargo; but, on its return, it was attacked by a number of vessels sent out by the Zamorin to intercept it, when a desperate battle ensued, though the skill and bravery of the Portugueze soon procured them a complete victory.

After the departure of Gama, the Zamorin, resolving to avenge himself on the rajah, for his assistance to the Portugueze, assembled an army of 50,000 men, and marched against Cochin. It was bravely defended by Vrimampara, the rajah, with a few chosen troops; but the superiority of the enemy's numbers having spread a general terror amongst the inhabitants of Cochin, they joined the Zamorin, and the place being taken without resistance, all who were found within its walls were put to the sword. The rajah had previously withdrawn his small force to the island of Vaypi, a short distance from the town, whither he had also sent all the Portugueze merchants; and, as this island had ever been rendered sacred to the Brahmins, it had hitherto been regarded with awe and reverence by all the Hindoo princes. The Zamorin, however, attacked it; but, by the enthusiasm of the troops within it, he was repulsed with great loss; and assistance having been sent to the rajah by the next annual fleet from Portugal, the recapture of Cochin was speedily effected.

The Portugueze, however, as their influence increased, insidiously and continually fomented disputes amongst the different princes; and, by always taking the strongest side, they obtained considerable grants of land, as the reward for their services. At length Emanuel, king of Portugal, who had hitherto acted with becoming spirit and prudence, formed the absurd design of expelling the Mahomedans from India; but the hostilities committed in the interim by the Mappilas, or Mahomedans of Malabar, against the Portugueze, required all his attention to preserve the possessions he had already gained. The forces, however, intended for religious warfare were not useless: several squadrons were sent in 1506 on voyages of research, and the result was the discovery of Madagascar and the Maladives, and the possession of Ceylon; when, by the expulsion of the Arabian merchants, the trade between this island and the Red Sea was annihilated to them, and reverted exclusively to the Portugueze, who now found themselves possessed of a greater extent of commercial power, than they had ever before attained. In consequence of this success the king of Portugal declared himself sovereign of the Indian Seas, sent out a governor with the pompous title of Viceroy of the Indies, and issued a decree, declaring, that if the ships of any nation dared to traverse those seas, without permission from the Portugueze admiral, they would be confiscated. This insolent order exasperating the Venetians and the Soldan of the Mamelukes, by the latter of which people the trade had long been carried on by way of the Red Sea, they jointly fitted out a formidable fleet, which was united with one prepared by the Arabs for the same expedition: it fell in with the Portugueze fleet off the island of Diu, under the command of the governor-general d'Almeyda, by whom it was totally defeated; and the result was the speedy conquest by the Portugueze, of every place on the coast between Diu and Cochin. This governor was succeeded by Albuquerque, who, with a view to get possession of the port of Calicut, declared war against the Zamorin, in which he was ultimately worsted. He then sailed with a strong force, and captured by storm the town of Goa. Elated by his success, he next proceeded against Malacca, which he likewise took by storm, together with property which he sold to the merchants of the place for 400,000l. sterling; but, on his return to Malabar, he lost the greater part of his fleet in a tempest, together with nearly all the spoils he had acquired.

His next achievement, after having received reinforcements, was the complete conquest of the island of Ormuz, in the Persian Gulf, without the loss of a man. A partial insurrection having broken out in that place, he availed himself of the confusion, and arrived there in six weeks after his departure from Goa; when, by intimidating Turrah Shah, the monarch, he induced him to acknowledge himself a vassal of the king of Portugal.

Thus the commercial and political fame of the Portugueze was extended through all the nations of Asia; and they derived no small advantage from the knowledge of those whom they subdued, that in their victorious career, they had committed as few cruelties or excesses as any conquerors recorded in history.

The death of Albuquerque, which happened at Goa, soon after the subjugation of Ormuz, together with that of Emanuel, in 1521, arrested for a time the successes of the Portugueze in the East. But they obtained a complete monopoly of the spice trade; and extending their discoveries to the eastward, soon began an intercourse with China and Japan, till at last they possessed a chain of settlements, which extended from Ceylon to the mouths of the Indus.

After the death of John III. in 1557, his successor, Sebastian, animated with a Jesuitical zeal, renewed the project of converting the whole of the inhabitants of India to the Catholic religion, and began by enlarging his ecclesiastical establishments in that country; deliberate and systematic cruelties were resorted to for the purpose of making proselytes; and the persecution was continued with unremitting fury during the short existence of this monarch, as well as of Don Henry, who succeeded him. But when Portugal was subjected in 1580, to Philip II. of Spain, the conduct of the Portugueze in India towards the natives was so intolerable, that they were involved with them for 60 years in perpetual contests. At length the Mahrattas, who were ever the most warlike people in India, disgusted at the enormities committed by these propagators of Christianity, marched against, and defeated them in every direction; and their ruin was finally completed by the Dutch, who finding both Portugal and Spain, from which latter monarchy they themselves had revolted, unable to send assistance to their valuable colonies, attacked them on every occasion, and in a few years conquered their spice islands, Ceylon, and many other tracts of inferior importance. The proximate causes, however, of the loss of those vast possessions, were the rage for propagating a new faith, and the inordinate avarice of individuals, who acquired enormous fortunes by every species of plunder and rapacity.

Before we quitted the political, to give an insight of the commercial, proceedings in Hindostan, we had carried the former subject down to the commencement of the 17th century, or to the close of the reign of the justly celebrated Akbar, whose possessions, at his death, extended from the mountains of Thebet on the north, to Visiapour and Golconda on the south; and from Aracan and Bootan on the east, to the river Attock and Cabulistan on the west:—a territory comprising 105 provinces, and 2737 districts, forming, on the whole, the richest, and most valuable part of India. He was, like all his predecessors, the absolute proprietor of the soil, the gross produce of which constituted the revenues of the government, while a sixth part of the whole had been claimed for ages by the prince. During the reign of Akbar, the encouragement he afforded to agriculture and the arts, caused the revenues to be more abundant than at any former period; for, on an average of the 26 years of his sovereignty, they amounted annually to 36,000,000l. sterling.—This income is derivable from what is called the Mogul empire, and was drawn principally from the gross produce of the land; while out of it was paid, in the provinces, the expenses of all the civil and military establishments, the latter of which is said, in the Ayeen Akbary, to have consisted in regular and irregular troops, of 4,000,000 men.—There was, however, no great difficulty in collecting it, nor much fluctuation in the average amount; for notwithstanding the continual wars in which the country was involved, the immense sums annually brought by the different nations for the purchase of Indian merchandize, and none of which, as we have before observed, was ever suffered to return, always contributed to keep in circulation an immense quantity of specie.—By this sketch, therefore, of the finances of the empire at the decline of the Portugueze power, though it has no particular connexion with the present history, an idea may be formed of the general importance of the country at the time of the establishment of the British East India Company.

It is asserted by William of Malmsbury, and Rymer in his

Fœdera, that Alfred the Great assisted several merchants with ships and money, to trade to Egypt, where they procured the commodities of India; but from his death to the time of Henry VIII. this country appears to have been supplied with them almost exclusively by the merchants of Venice.—After the discovery of the passage by the Cape, the merchants of London imported their Indian goods from Lisbon; and though a Mr. Thorn presented a memorial to Henry on the subject of opening a direct commerce with India, it is singular that that ambitious monarch never gave it the smallest encouragement. In the reign of Elizabeth, however, a commercial treaty was entered into between this country and Turkey, in consequence of which the English merchants obtained great privileges in the Turkish ports, and brought to England, in their own ships, the Indian goods which had been conveyed to Europe by way of Egypt. This method, however, did not produce the desired effect; for the English merchants were undersold by the Dutch: in consequence of which those of London confederated, for the purpose of trading direct to India; and, on application to the queen, they obtained a charter for the East India Company. They then learned that her majesty had formed the same comprehensive project in her own mind; and that in order to forward her views, she had six months before sent Mr. Mildenhall, the consul at Constantinople, over land to India, with letters to the emperor Akbar, for the purpose of procuring privileges for the English merchants. Rymer asserts that he returned to England without success, though it is certain that he was extremely well received by Akbar.

The queen, however, fully aware of the vast importance of the speculation, did not wait to ascertain the result of this mission; but, about six months after the departure of Mildenhall from Constantinople, she granted a charter for instituting the East India Company. It was made to George, earl of Cumberland, and 215 knights, aldermen, and merchants, which formed a body politic and corporate, under the title of the Governor and Company of Merchants of London, trading to the East Indies. The principal features of this charter are, that a governor and 24 directors shall be chosen annually by the Company; that the directors shall form committees, who shall have the regulation of the voyages, the sale of the merchandise, and the general management of all the Company's affairs. That the freedom of trading, to all the ports of India, shall be granted for 15 years to them and their heirs; to their sons, when of age, and to such apprentices, servants, and factors, as might be employed by them. That they might make bye laws; inflict legal punishment; export goods free of duty for four years, and to export to the amount of 30,000l. in foreign bullion, provided that 6000l. of it were re-coined in this country. The exclusive right of trading to India was allowed to them, and was prohibited under severe penalties, to all other British subjects; but, to guard against an injurious monopoly of the trade, government reserved to itself the privilege of stopping it, at any period within the 15 years allowed by the charter, on giving two years notice. On obtaining these privileges the Company, to execute their projects, proceeded to raise a sum of money, which soon amounted to 72,000l. with which they equipped their first trading fleet, consisting of one ship of 600 tons, one of 300, one of 200, and a provision ship of 180 tons. This fleet sailed with a cargo of bullion, muskets, cutlasses, &c. to the value of 27,000l. under the command of captain Lancaster, who had previously made an unsuccessful voyage in a ship of his own. On the 13th of February, 1601, it left the Downs for Acheen, in Sumatra; to the king of which island Elizabeth had sent letters, with an offer to conclude a treaty of commerce. After a long and disagreeable voyage of 15 months and a half, they arrived at Acheen, and were on the next day received by the king with great ceremony. He appeared highly pleased with the presents sent by the queen, the principal of which was a fan of feathers. He then gave a sumptuous banquet to the officers, and the treaty was concluded on the most favourable terms. This object being accomplished, captain Lancaster took in a cargo of pepper, and sailed for Bantam, in Java: on his way he captured a Portugueze ship, richly laden with spices. At Bantam he met with a reception as flattering as at Acheen; and, after obtaining the same privileges as he had gained at the latter place, he sailed for England, where he arrived in September, 1603.

The success of this expedition, together with the patronage afforded to the Company by James I. who had just ascended the throne, diffused an unexampled degree of vigour amongst the merchants; and, in the spring of 1604, they dispatched a second fleet of three ships, under sir H. Middleton, who bore letters to the different princes of India; before his return, a third fleet was sent out under sir E. Michelbourn, both of which arrived in safety, and the former returned to Portsmouth in June, 1606. In the mean time, however, the Dutch, at all the ports to which our ships were destined, endeavoured to prejudice the natives against the English, by every insiduous artifice; and, as the prosperity and influence of the latter increased, the enmity of the former became extensive and undisguised; so that frequent hostilities took place in the islands. But James, being anxious to avoid a war with any foreign state, refused to remonstrate with the Dutch government on the improper conduct of their agents, though he granted a more enlarged charter to the Company; and a new expedition was equipped, in which was a ship of 1200 tons, for the purpose of proceeding to the ports on the continent of India, as well as to the eastern Archipelago. At Mocha, sir H. Middleton, the commander of this squadron, having had an affray with the natives, was thrown in chains into a dungeon, and threatened with torture unless he gave up his ships, which, however, he resolutely refused to do, and some months afterwards he made his escape. On regaining his ships, which had been kept in the harbour, he threatened to lay the town in ashes, unless the remainder of the prisoners were set at liberty, and a handsome remuneration given to him for his sufferings; which so intimidated the Arabs, that they immediately acceded to his demands. He then proceeded to India, and found at the mouth of the river of Surat, a Portugueze fleet of six men of war and 12 gallies, stationed there for the purpose of preventing any other nation from trading to that port. Being however joined by six merchant vessels from the port of Sually, he boldly dashed into the midst of the enemy's fleet; and, by his well-directed fire, threw them into such consternation, that several of their largest ships were taken by boarding, while the rest made a precipitate retreat. The Jesuit influence, however, prevented him from gaining any advantage at Surat: he therefore returned to the Red Sea, and captured on his passage several Portugueze vessels, together with a fleet of 18 sail from India, bound to Mocha. Shortly after this affair he proceeded to Bantam, where he died.

As it would be impossible to trace in our circumscribed limits the gradual rise and progress of the Company, we shall proceed to record some signal advantages, which were acquired by our forces, at various periods; premising, that the affairs of our merchants continued so prosperous, that in 1612, their joint stock amounted to 150,000l. and they regularly dispatched a merchant fleet to India every spring. The good faith observed by the English contributed much to promote their interests, and procured them the favour of many of the native princes, who had become disgusted with the duplicity of the Dutch and Portugueze.

In 1613, captain Best, with four ships of 30 guns each, was attacked off Surat by a large armament fitted out by the Portugueze viceroy at Goa, consisting of four large galleons and 26 frigates, with 5000 men, and 130 pieces of heavy ordnance. The action continued for eight hours with the most resistless fury; after which, the Portugueze fleet was obliged to retreat to Goa with the greatest precipitation. This was followed by another complete victory over the same fleet, which had been refitted at Goa; and thus the English obtained an undisputed maritime sovereignty in those seas, which they have ever since maintained.

Before he returned to Europe, Best fully attained the great objects he had in view, by gaining the favour of the Mogul emperor, who allowed the English to establish a factory at Surat, and to enjoy every commercial advantage throughout his empire. Proceeding next to Acheen, the king of that territory renewed his charter with the company, and granted them additional privileges; after which captain Best arrived safely at London, with a valuable cargo of spices, and received many distinguished marks of approbation.

The success of this last expedition gave additional vigour to the exertions of the Company; who, wishing to profit by the high opinion entertained of them by the people of India, they suggested the propriety of sending out a splendid embassy to the Mogul, with a special commission to conclude a more general treaty of commerce with that sovereign. James, who had always been favourably disposed towards the Company, consented to their proposal, and appointed sir Thomas Roe, as his ambassador extraordinary to India.

The magnificent presents, and other appendages of the embassy being in readiness, sir Thomas sailed in March, 1614, for Surat, where he landed, after a voyage of six months. As soon as his arrival was known, the emperor sent a vakeel to conduct him to his residence at Ajmeer, where he was received with greater pomp and magnificence, than had ever before been witnessed, even in an Oriental court. He resided there seven months, and at length concluded a treaty highly favourable to the Company, but not equal to his own wishes; as the prime minister of Jehangeer, the Mogul listening to the insinuations of the Portugueze, excited a degree of suspicion in the mind of that monarch, relative to the intent of the English, which it was difficult to overcome. They, however, by this treaty, obtained leave to send agents to Surat, Sually, Baroach, and many other parts of the empire, and thus they soon completely turned the Oriental commerce in their favour; the Portugueze having, before the close of the 17th century, been nearly expelled, and the Dutch only retaining possession of the Spice Islands.

It is necessary here to observe, that in the commercial history of India, no nation appears to have made such a rapid and successful progress as the Dutch. Having long been accustomed to procure the commodities of the East from Lisbon, it is not surprising that the ardent and emulous disposition of that people should have led them to attempt the establishment of a trade of their own. Accordingly, towards the close of the 16th century, we find them making the most extraordinary efforts to fit out ships for the Indian seas; and though they at first encountered unparalleled difficulties, they were not disheartened, but continued their enterprises with unremitting activity. Having freed themselves from the oppressive shackles of Spain, the restraints which had been imposed upon their speculative ardour gave way before the spontaneous exertions of their indefatigable industry; and, in 1594, they attempted to execute their favourite project of sailing to China by the Northern Ocean, which they hoped would prove a much shorter passage than that of the Cape, and that they should thus be enabled to supply the European markets with the produce of India, at a far lower rate than could be afforded by their competitors. A small squadron was accordingly dispatched, under the command of William Barentz, a distinguished navigator, who sailed from Amsterdam in the beginning of 1596; but, on reaching the latitude of 78 degrees, his squadron was surrounded by mountains of ice; and his crew, alarmed at their situation, insisted on returning to Holland, with whose demand he was obliged to comply; and he arrived in the Texel after an absence of five months. Barentz, however, was held in such high estimation by the States, that, on his own proposition, he was again employed to discover a north-east passage by the Straits of Wygatz, and sailed for the North Seas in June, 1596. The Dutch government, and indeed the whole nation, were extremely sanguine concerning this expedition; but their hopes were proportionately disappointed by the return of Barentz, at the end of four months, without having made any new discovery.

The Dutch then turned all their attention to the navigation round the Cape of Good Hope; and on receiving an application from Cornelius Houtman, an enterprising Dutchman, who was at that time imprisoned in Lisbon by the Portugueze government, on suspicion of favouring the interests of his countrymen, they resolved to procure his liberty, which they did by paying a considerable sum of money to his oppressors. On his arrival at Amsterdam, his information appeared of such importance, that a company of merchants was immediately formed in that city; and, in less than three months, or in the autumn of 1596, a squadron of four ships sailed, under the command of Houtman, direct for the eastern Archipelago, which, after a passage of nine months, anchored off Bantam. The inhabitants of Java received the Dutch commander with great courtesy, and Houtman had already begun to take in a cargo of spices; but, suspecting that the Malay merchants had given him goods of an inferior quality, he rashly remonstrated with the king, who ordered him to be thrown into a dungeon; and he only saved himself from assassination, by offering as a ransom to the tyrant, a part of the money appropriated to the purchase of his cargo. He then secretly left Bantam with his fleet, and arrived in the Texel towards the end of 1598.

The importance of having opened a direct intercourse with the East, caused the merchants to feel little disappointment at the return of their ships in a great degree empty; but, in the beginning of 1599, they sent out another squadron, consisting of eight ships, under the command of Houtman and Van-Neck, which arrived at Acheen, in Sumatra, towards the end of that year: they also dispatched a squadron of four ships to the southern parts of Java; while the enterprising company at Rotterdam sent out another of five ships, under James Mahu, a native of Antwerp, by the hazardous passage of the Straits of Magellan: this commander, after encountering imminent danger, and losing two of his vessels, reached the Moluccas in 19 months.

These, and subsequent expeditions, proved highly successful; and, in the short space of five years, the Dutch trade with India had so prodigiously increased, that in 1600, they sent out 40 ships, from 400 to 600 tons burthen, which procured them an almost entire monopoly of the spice trade.

During the rapid advancement of their trade with the Indian isles, the Dutch were involved in frequent and serious disputes with the natives, and were in almost incessant warfare with the Spaniards and Portugueze, who, foreseeing the certain annihilation of their own commerce in the successful enterprises of their rivals, resorted to every kind of treachery and duplicity, in order to prejudice the islanders against their new intruders. On the other hand, the Dutch retorted, by secretly representing, that the Portugueze had come to India more in the character of warriors than in that of merchants, and that their real object was to reduce the natives to slavery, and force them to abjure the religion of Mahomed; while their own gentle manners tended to give much plausibility to their assertions. The consequence was, a speedy expulsion from the Moluccas of all the Portugueze settlers; and, at Acheen, so vindictive were the Malays, that, having stormed a small fortress belonging to the Portugueze, at the bottom of the bay, they massacred every European who was found within it. The Dutch, who were in reality the instigators of these outrages, did not fail to turn them to their own advantage, and succeeded in obtaining exclusively from the inhabitants of Celebes, Ternate, and the Moluccas, all the finest aromatics which those islands produced.

The intelligence of these events did not fail to excite the most violent animosity of Philip of Spain against the Dutch, and his first effort was to send out all the armed ships of Spain and Portugal, with a view to intercept the next squadron, that they might send to India. The combined fleet, consisting of 30 ships, proceeded towards Cape Verd; and, in May, 1601, fell in with a Dutch fleet of eight Indiamen, each of which, though unprepared for war, carried 16 small guns, and 60 men. Notwithstanding this great disparity, the Dutch commander, Spilbergan, resolved to fight his way through the enemy's line; and the Spanish and Portugueze fleets endeavouring to surround that of Spilbergan in three divisions, fell into such confusion, that, after an action of two hours, they were obliged to retire, while the Dutch triumphantly pursued their voyage.

In the mean time, the Portugueze governors in India not being able to procure reinforcements from their own country; and knowing, by experience, that from the growing influence of their cotemporaries, they would soon be driven from every spot they possessed, resorted again to artifice; and, in their turn, prejudiced the Malays against the Dutch commanders, then at Acheen, amongst whom was the celebrated Houtman:—the latter soon perceiving in the king an uncommon degree of coolness, demanded an explanation; but, obtaining no answer, he returned to his ship. On the following night his vessel was surrounded by a number of armed proas, who endeavoured to board; but, after a desperate conflict of two hours, they were defeated with great slaughter, though the Dutch in this affair lost their gallant commander. Shortly after this event, Spilbergan arrived at Acheen, and forced the king not only to make the most humble acknowledgment for the outrage, but to renew the commercial relations which had proved so advantageous to his country.

The success of the Dutch having for some time after this event been uninterrupted, their markets were overstocked with the produce of India; and, to prevent its depreciation, they were under the necessity of joining the funds of their different companies into one body corporate, which, in March, 1602, received a patent for 21 years, under the title of "The Dutch East India Company."—Their whole stock consisted of 6,600,000 guilders, or about 600,000l. This effort gave new vigour to their operations; and, in June, 1602, they sent out a fleet to India, consisting of 14 sail, under admiral Van Waerwyk, which arrived in safety at the Moluccas, and was soon followed by another of 13 sail, under Vander Hagen, who had on board a considerable body of troops. With this force he invested the Portugueze settlements at Amboyna and Tidore, and captured them, together with a number of vessels, which were lying in the harbour, richly laden. Thus the whole of the possessions of the Portugueze in the Moluccas fell into the hands of the Dutch; and which, notwithstanding many attempts, with partial success, they were never able to regain.

Pursuing their views of aggrandizement, the Dutch next formed an alliance with the king of Candy, which had for its object the expulsion of the Portugueze from Ceylon; and a squadron under De Weert having fallen in with, and defeated one belonging to Portugal, near the settlement of Negombo, he proceeded to Battacola, the principal port of the king of Candy, with his prizes.

On appearing before the king, a serious misunderstanding arose respecting the kind treatment by De Weert of the Portugueze prisoners; and accusations having been made against the Dutch commander, of the non-performance of his treaty, he resented it in so explicit a manner, that the king ordered him to be seized, and thrown into a dungeon. The brave admiral refused to submit to this treatment, and defended himself for some time with his sword; till, being overpowered by numbers, he was struck dead by a blow from a scimitar. By this event the crews of the Dutch fleet were panic struck; and the Portugueze being about to take advantage of their rupture with the Candians, in order to attack them, they were obliged to sail with precipitation from Battacola for Amboyna, where their settlements were in a very precarious state.

It would be impossible, in our brief limits, to describe the particulars of every naval and military action, which took place in the Indian seas, and islands, between the Dutch and their inveterate rivals, the Portugueze and Spaniards, till their attainment of that high state of commercial prosperity, which rendered them the most opulent merchants of Europe. The vicissitudes of fortune were rapid, and for several years the Dutch in India were surrounded by enemies; they, however, maintained the good opinion of the natives, by gaining frequent victories over the squadrons of Portugal and Spain, in the Indian seas; and their success was finally completed by assisting the king of Candy, in 1612, to repel a serious invasion of the Portugueze, who had advanced within a few miles of his capital. The invaders were repulsed entirely by the judicious conduct of Boshkoveur, the Dutch naval commander; and, in return for this service, his nation received a grant of those extensive and valuable establishments in Ceylon, which have lately reverted to Great Britain. In 1617, they obtained equal advantages at Bantam, where they were allowed to build a factory; while their possessions in the eastern seas were so numerous, that they extended over the greatest part of the Archipelago. At Siam, and Japan, they also possessed factories; and, in 1622, they had built the magnificent city of Batavia, which was made the seat of government for the Dutch possessions in that quarter of the world.

The great commercial rivalry on the continent of Asia, however, principally rested at this period, as well as for a century afterwards, between Britain and France; though the views of the latter were not fully developed till after the peace of Aix la Chapelle, at which time the possessions of the French were of considerable extent. The British, also, at this time, had settlements at Surat, Bombay, Dabul, Carwar, Tellicherry, Anjengo, Tegapatan, Madras, Vizagapatam, Balagore, and Calcutta. The French possessed Chandernagore and Pondicherry.

The first war in India, between the French and English, originated in the intrigues of Dupleix, commander of the French troops; who, in 1747, having assisted Muzaphier Sing, cousin of Nazir Sing, nabob of the Carnatic, in a rebellion against his relative, the English were obliged to assist the latter with a force under colonel Laurence. Dupleix, however, withdrew his troops in the night, which obliged his ally to surrender. Nazir Sing spared his enemy's life, in return for which he was secretly murdered by the traitor in his tent; and the immense plunder found in the camp was mostly seized by Dupleix, who immediately assumed the authority of the prince, and appointed Chunda Saib, a colleague of Muzaphier, to be nabob of Arcot; the real nabob, Anaverdy Khan, having been murdered by these confederates in 1749. The English government took the part of the son of Anaverdy; and, being aided by several other nabobs, Muzaphier was defeated, and put to death. Chunda Saib, however, by large promises to Dupleix, obtained from him 4000 sepoys, and about 500 French, with which force he conquered Anaverdy, regained the government, and ceded to the French the town of Velur and its dependencies, consisting of 45 villages. In the mean time, Mahomed Ali Khan, son of Anaverdy Khan, having been protected and assisted by the British, made them several important cessions; and, being seconded by a force under Mr. Clive, who had till then been a writer in the Company's service, the enemy were entirely defeated by the latter on the plains of Arcani, in December, 1751. In 1752, Mr. Clive, with 300 Europeans, and as many natives, defeated, near Arcot, a body of the enemy, consisting of 1500 sepoys, 1700 cavalry, and 150 Frenchmen, with eight pieces of artillery. The whole of the French surrendered on this occasion, and their baggage and cannon fell into our possession. Mr. Clive soon afterwards cut off the retreat of the French to Pondicherry, and captured their whole force, with d'Anteuil their commander. Chunda Saib, who had an army of 3000 men near Tritchinopoly, passing about the same time through

Tanjore, fell into the hands of the nabob, who struck off his head, and his army was totally routed by major Laurence. Dupleix, however, instead of abandoning his schemes, assumed the rank of an Indian prince, and produced forged commissions, pretending that the Mogul had appointed him governor of the Carnatic.

Thus a series of hostilities was continued between the French and English Companies till Dupleix was recalled; and M. Gadeheu, his successor, concluded a treaty, the basis of which was, that neither of the Companies should in future interfere in any disturbances amongst the native princes. But the French, pursuing their systematic duplicity, endeavoured, immediately after the signing of this treaty, to get possession of the fortress of Golconda, and all the provinces in the Deccan; and they even sent a force to the country of the Polygars, to induce them to resist paying their tribute, which was divided between the nabob and the English Company. This brought on a renewal of hostilities; and the English, after reducing the refractory Polygars, captured the strong town of Madura, about 60 miles from Tritchinopoly, when a neighbouring Polygar prince offered them two settlements on the coast opposite to Ceylon. Favoured by this acquisition, the English army, under colonel Heron, captured Coilgoody, and Tinevelly:—at a fort, called Nellecotta, it is said that he barbarously refused quarter to the garrison, and massacred 400 men, women, and children. He was soon afterwards disgraced for misconduct, in suffering the baggage of the English to be surprised by the natives in the pass of Natam.

In March, 1755, a very important advantage was gained by a few vessels under commodore James, who attacked and destroyed the possessions of Tulagee Angria, a Mahratta pirate, who had long done the most serious injury to the commerce of the Europeans. This chief possessed several islands near Bombay, and an extent of coast nearly 180 miles in length, while his successes had struck such terror into the European sailors, that in 1754, he captured with his small vessels, two Dutch frigates and a sloop.

Until the expedition of commodore James, the Company had been obliged to keep up a naval force, to protect their trade, at an expense of 50,000l. per annum; but the commodore attacked Gerrah, the capital of the abovementioned pirate, with so much success, that he fled to the Mahrattas, and the English took possession of the place, in which they found 200 pieces of brass cannon, a quantity of ammunition, and property to the amount of 125,000l.

Our countrymen, however, were doomed to a continued continental warfare, for in 1756, Suraja Dowla, the new nabob of Arcot, and grandson of Anaverdy Khan, having found a pretence for war in the repairs made by the English at the fortifications of Calcutta, entered the field on the 30th May, with an army of 40,000 infantry, 30,000 cavalry, and 400 elephants. He first invested the English fort at Cassimbuzar with 20,000 men, and elated by its surrender, he immediately proceeded to invest Calcutta:—here he proposed an accommodation, provided the English government would pay him his duty upon the trade for 15 years, deliver up the Indian merchants in the fort, and defray the expenses of his numerous army;

which being refused, he captured that place, after a siege of three days, principally by the treachery of the Dutch guard, who opened the gates to the besiegers. The nabob, in revenge, although he had promised that no injury should be done to the garrison, no sooner entered the place, than he ordered all the English to be shut up in a sort of cave, called the Black-hole; where, out of 146, only 22 were found alive the next morning.—In consequence of this disaster, colonel Clive was sent to Bengal, on board admiral Watson's fleet, with about 1000 sepoys and 400 Europeans, with whom he landed at Fulta, and subdued the forts Busbudgia, Tauna, Fort William, and Calcutta, as well as the large town of Hoogly, which was filled with the richest merchandize. A successful attack was next made on the camp of Suraja Dowla, which induced him, in February, 1757, to conclude a treaty, by which the English gained very considerable advantages.

Scarcely had this contest terminated in the East, when news was received of a war between England and France, and the reduction of the French power again became an object of importance; but the nabob, Suraja Dowla, informed the council of Bengal, that if hostilities were carried into his country by the English, he would assist the French with all his power. Admiral Watson, in reply, wished the nabob to guarantee a treaty of neutrality on the part of the French; which he refused to do, in consequence of the latter having persuaded him, that after the subjugation of Chandernagore, the English would turn their arms against himself. Hostilities were then commenced; and, after a vigorous assault, in resisting which the French displayed great bravery, Chandernagore was taken; and the nabob having shewn marks of displeasure at this event, it was resolved to depose him, by supporting Meer Jaffier Ali Khan, who had married the sister of Aliverdy Khan, Suraja's predecessor. The army destined to effect this revolution marched under colonel Clive, on the 13th of June; and, on reaching the nabob's frontiers, the colonel sent him a letter, which upbraided him for his conduct, and concluded with observing, that the rains being about to commence, he had found it necessary to wait on him immediately. This was followed by a decisive action in the plains of Plassay, in which the nabob's troops were routed in every direction, and he was obliged to fly from his capital in the disguise of a faquir. He was accompanied by two attendants, who robbed him on the road; and being found two days afterwards in the most miserable state, he was brought to Muxadabad, and beheaded by Meer Jaffier's eldest son. The usurper was then declared, by colonel Clive, the lawful nabob of Bengal.

As soon as this affair had been concluded, major Coote was dispatched with a body of sepoys, in pursuit of some French prisoners who had escaped from Chandernagore, and the advantages which resulted from this expedition are too considerable to be passed over in silence. He compelled Ramnarin, a powerful rajah, to swear allegiance to Meer Jaffier, and discovered the process employed in his territories for making saltpetre, which has since been of the utmost consequence to this country.

On the 16th August, 1757, admiral Watson died, to the great

regret of all the British residents in India. He was succeeded by admiral Pococke. In this month the success of the British appeared to turn; as the French under Bussy, and those who had escaped under Law, from Chandernagore, formed a junction; and, by the conquest of Vizagapatam, and other posts, became masters of all the coast from Ganjam to Masulipatam, together with several of the English factories in that direction: in the southern provinces, also, the rebel Polygars defeated Mazuphe Khan, and conquered the city of Madura. It was, however, after an unsuccessful attempt to reduce it, purchased by the English in 1758, for 170,000 rupees. The whole campaign of this year proved unfavourable, as our force was reduced at its termination to 1718 men, while that of the French amounted to 3400, exclusive of natives.

Some victories were nevertheless gained at sea by admiral Pococke, who defeated the French naval force on the 24th of March, and 3d of August, with great loss on their side, and but little on our own. By land general Lally retaliated, by reducing and destroying Fort St. David, and committing the most shocking ravages in the neighbouring villages:—but the general indignation excited by his conduct caused him to be defeated before Tanjore, and from that time several of his enterprises were equally unsuccessful.

On the 10th of September, 1759, admiral Pococke defeated the French a third time, though the number of their ships and men was infinitely superior to ours. The enemy had 1500 men killed and wounded, while our loss did not exceed 569.—After this victory admiral Pococke returned to England.

The defeat of the French by sea had now thrown a damp on the spirits of their land troops, which they could not recover; and, on the 22d of January, 1760, they mustered all their force near Wandewash, and risked a general action with colonel Coote, who had an army of only 1700 Europeans, and 3000 natives, while that of the French amounted to 2200 Europeans, and 10,300 blacks, with a proportionate superiority of cannon. In three hours, however, they were totally defeated, and obliged to retreat with the utmost rapidity to Pondicherry. This disaster was followed by the speedy conquest of all the French forts in India, and finally by the reduction of Pondicherry, which capitulated on the 15th January, 1761; and thus the French power in the East was for some time annihilated.

It is a lamentable reflection, that the English, by their insidious policy, and tyrannical conduct in the East, have on many occasions tarnished the lustre of their most glorious achievements. On the subjugation of the French, they ravaged every acre of territory between Wandewash and Pondicherry, in revenge for a similar outrage of the enemy near Madras; and afterwards, finding that Meer Jaffier, the person whom they had made nabob of Bengal, by the destruction of Suraja Dowla, was unable to pay the enormous exactions they had levied upon him, they brought forward a variety of frivolous charges and accusations, some of which had not a shadow of evidence; and, in violation of the most solemn treaty, he was secretly surrounded in his palace by a corps under colonel Caillaud, when, being forced into a boat with a part of his family and some jewels, he was sent off to Calcutta. The actors in this infamous affair then placed Meer Cossim Khan on the musnud, and afterwards had the effrontery to declare, that they had been promised 20 lacks of rupees in the event of his success, which was to be secured by the assassination of Meer Jaffier, whose mild disposition had procured him general esteem.

Meer Cossim, however, was a very different character from his predecessor; and, profiting by experience, resolved to rid himself of the shackles of the Company as speedily as possible. With this view he removed his capital from Muxadabad to Mongheer, about 200 miles farther from Calcutta, which he fortified, and formed in it a garrison of Armenian and Tartarian troops, together with all the sepoys who had been dismissed from the English service. With these he endeavoured to discipline his Indian army, and soon raised a formidable train of artillery. When his project was sufficiently matured, he began to abolish the immunities paid by Jaffier to the Company; and having, at his accession, ceded territories to the English worth 700,000l. a year, besides other revenues, amounting to 70,000l. per annum, he insisted that he had a right to remunerate himself, by subjecting the English traders in his dominions to certain duties. On this Mr. Vansittart was sent by the government of Calcutta to remonstrate; but this gentleman was so disconcerted by a threat of Cossim to lay open the trade entirely to all nations, and thus ruin the private commerce of the British factory, that he entered into a treaty, by which the English trade was submitted to certain restrictions. The government at Calcutta, however, refused to ratify it, and immediately commenced hostilities.

The first attack was made at Patna, a city about 300 miles from Calcutta, in which the English had a fortified factory, with a small European force. These troops, however, surprised the city, which had a strong garrison; but not taking the necessary precautions to secure themselves, it was recaptured in a few hours, and all the English were put to the sword. This act stimulated Cossim to perpetrate others far more perfidious; for the council of Calcutta having sent some deputies, with Mr. Amyatt at their head, to treat for a new commercial agreement, and thus effect a reconciliation, he was waylaid near Muxadabad, and the whole of his party cut to pieces. The council then thought proper again to declare Meer Jaffier, whom they had deposed, to be nabob of Bengal; and major Adams, with only one regiment of the line, some sepoys, and 12 pieces of cannon, gained several victories over the natives, particularly near Cassimbuzar, a branch of the Ganges, where they defeated 10,000 of Cossim's troops, and captured a fort defended by entrenchments 15 feet high, with many pieces of artillery. Pursuing their victorious career with reinforcements, they attacked, on the 2d August, 1763, the main forces of the Indian army on the banks of the Nunas Nullas; and, after an obstinate battle of four hours, obliged them to retire with the loss of all their cannon. The enemy's troops on this occasion amounted to 20,000 horse and 8000 foot.

Mongheer, the capital of Cossim, was then subdued, after a siege of nine days; and this tyrant, in a paroxysm of despair, retaliated by ordering the massacre of all the prisoners taken at Patna. For this purpose, a German assassin, named Somers, was hired, who invited the English to an entertainment, and placed a party on the top of the house to fire down upon them as they entered, while others were seized, and murdered in a manner still more barbarous. The prisoners amounted to about 200 in number, none of whom were saved, except Dr. Fullarton, who had received a pardon from Meer Cossim, a few days before the execution of this sanguinary project. It should be added, to the honour of the natives, that they at first refused to fire upon the prisoners, unless the latter were furnished with arms, on which Somers run several of them through the body!

The English next besieged Patna, which surrendered in eight days; and Meer Cossim having no longer any place capable of resistance, fled to Suja Dowla, nabob of Oude, leaving our forces in possession of the whole of Bengal.

After Meer Jaffier, the deposed nabob, had been restored by the Company to his throne, they attempted to form an alliance with the abovementioned nabob of Oude, which he scornfully rejected: hostilities were consequently resolved on against him, and colonel H. Munro was appointed to succeed major Adams, who died soon after the conquest of Patna. Meer Cossim assisted the nabob, took the command of his forces; and, having fallen in with a party of English, put them to death, and sent their heads to Suja Dowla. Having then under his command an army of 50,000 men, with a proportionate train of artillery, he again resolved to risk a general action with the English; and, on the 22d of October, 1764, the engagement took place at Buxard, about 100 miles above Patna. Victory was firmly contested, and at length terminated in favour of the English, who lost in killed and wounded only 90 Europeans, and 700 natives, while the enemy had 6000 killed, and lost 130 pieces of cannon.

Several forts were then successively taken by colonel Munro; and the Mogul, to whom Suja Dowla was grand vizier, having concluded a treaty with the English, the lastmentioned officer was compelled to make an abject surrender, after sustaining another defeat by general Carnac, near Calpi. Before his surrender he permitted the escape of Meer Cossim, and Somers, the assassin, and neither threats nor intreaties could induce him to disclose the place of their retreat.

In February, 1765, Meer Jaffier, the nabob of Bengal, died, and the succession being disputed between his eldest surviving son, Najem ul Dowla, and a grandson of his eldest son Miran, deceased, who was then only seven years old, the council of Calcutta decreed, that Najem should succeed his father, on condition of paying to the Company the annual sum of 800,000l.; that he should receive, as prime minister, a person appointed by the council; and that he should bind himself to pay due attention to the complaints of this assembly, against any of his officers. The nabob accepted the degrading conditions.

By this and numerous proceedings of a similar nature, the council of Calcutta had alarmed their superiors at home, who at length found it necessary to send out a governor general with unlimited powers; and this great appointment was conferred upon lord Clive, who arrived at Calcutta on the 3d of May, 1765. His first act, as is generally the case with men in power, was to undo what had been done by his predecessors, the council, and to place Suja Dowla again in the possession of his dominions; but the new financial regulations which he adopted, tended rather to embarrass than to enrich the Company; and though the extent of their territory was equal to that of the largest kingdom in Europe, their affairs were in such a distracted state, that government thought proper to subject the province of Bengal to the authority of the crown. About this period, also, they were involved in fresh difficulties by the arts of Hyder Ally, who had in some manner risen from the rank of a sepoy to that of a prince; and who, justly considering the English influence as a bar to his ambition, had induced the Nizam of the Deccan to make war against them. Hyder shortly took the field; but, being defeated in September, 1767, by colonel Smith, near Errour, he was deserted by the Nizam, who made a separate treaty with the English, and ceded to them the duanny of the Balegat Carnatic, as the price of his duplicity.

During the remainder of that year, the war was removed by Hyder to the mountainous country, while a detachment from Bombay captured his principal sea-port, Mangalore, with nine ships in the harbour; but the place was soon retaken. Hyder, on the other hand, derived great advantage from some disorders resulting from the appointment of field deputies in the British army, to controul the commander in chief, a practice which was attended with such corruption, and created such disgust, that several of our officers deserted to the enemy, and many forts were given up which might have made a strong resistance. The subsequent conduct of these deputies, who prevented general Smith from proceeding against Hyder's capital, when he had conquered nearly the whole of his territories, gave the enemy an opportunity of collecting his forces; and, after ravaging the country of the nabob of Arcot, the most faithful ally of the English, he obliged them to confine their operations to the defence of the Carnatic. He also obtained an incredible number of adventurers by his success in partial, without risking general engagements; and, in a short time, he was in possession of 90,000 cavalry. He was, however, attacked at a fort called Mulwaggle, by colonel Wood; who, with 460 Europeans, and 2300 sepoys, defeated a force of 14,000 horse, 12,000 infantry, and six battalions of sepoys. But the war still continued to the disadvantage of the Company; and Hyder at last appearing suddenly before Madras, occasioned so much alarm, that a treaty was concluded with him on the 3d April, 1769, which merely comprised the restoration of the places taken by both armies, and an agreement that each party should assist the other, when attacked by their respective enemies.

But it appears that the presidency of Madras soon proved the insincerity of their intentions; for Hyder Ally becoming involved in a war with the Mahrattas, they several times refused him the stipulated assistance, which excited in him an implacable hatred against the English, that was never afterwards overcome: he consequently applied for assistance to the French government, who seconded his views with the utmost dispatch, and thus enabled him to defeat the Mahrattas, and conclude a treaty with them upon the most advantageous terms.

The Mahrattas now, in their turn, became the most decided enemies of the English, and their animosity originated in the following circumstances. A dispute having arisen amongst the descendants of the rajah of Berar, and Rogonaut Row, respecting their pretensions to the dignity of Peishwa, or Ram Rajah, the latter murdered Narain Row, who had been confided to his care by Mada Row, the deceased Peishwa, and fled to Bombay, where, the justice of his cause not being at all investigated, he was protected by the English. This event occasioned not only the resentment of Hyder Ally, but a confederation of most of the princes of India, who seemed resolved to expel from their country, those whom they considered as the most faithless of European intruders. Hyder, therefore, soon assembled an army of 100,000 men; and, with a body of French troops under count de Lally, proceeded against Madras. These were to be opposed by only 1500 Europeans and 4200 sepoys, under sir H. Munro, who marched towards Conjeveram, where Hyder's troops were stationed, expecting to join a detachment under colonel Baillie. Hyder, however, had dispatched his son, Tippoo Saib, to cut off this lastmentioned detachment, with 30,000 horse, 8000 foot, and 12 pieces of cannon; but the brave handful of troops, under colonel Baillie, repulsed this immense force of the enemy with great slaughter, and succeeded in joining sir Hector on the 9th of September, though they were exposed to a galling fire from the whole of the enemy's artillery.

Intelligence was now received, that Hyder was advancing with his whole force to the assistance of his son; and, having fallen in with colonel Baillie's detachment, he opened upon his small party nearly 70 pieces of cannon. Perhaps there never was a more distinguished defence than that of our troops on this occasion: they repulsed his main body several times; and it was not till he had been joined by Tippoo Saib, that he could make any impression upon the British line. But this event at last taking place, in consequence of an irresistible superiority of numbers, colonel Baillie withdrew the remainder of his force to an eminence, where, though without ammunition, they repulsed the enemy 13 separate times; and, after losing 700 Europeans, the colonel received offers of quarter, provided the remaining force grounded their arms. This, however, was no sooner complied with, than the barbarian troops rushed upon them, and began an indiscriminate massacre, in which they were only checked by the honourable and resolute interference of the French commanders, Lally and Pimoran. The effect of this gallant resistance upon Hyder was so great, that he ever after regarded the English with a degree of apprehension bordering upon terror.

In consequence of the disaster of colonel Baillie, sir Eyre Coote was solicited, by the supreme council of Bengal, to take upon him the management of the war, to which he consented; and, from that moment, the balance turned decidedly in our favour. Hyder now changed his plan of operations, by detaching parties to besiege the principal forts of the Company; but, finding himself closely pursued by sir Eyre, he once more resolved to try the event of a pitched battle. With this intent he assembled an army of 40,000 cavalry, and 15,000 sepoys, with other troops, which made his whole force amount to 200,000 men. On the 1st of July, 1781, a dreadful battle took place, and lasted from nine in the morning till four in the afternoon, when the English, after experiencing a most obstinate resistance, gained a complete victory; but, owing to a want of cavalry, they were prevented from following up their success. Hyder now appeared in a state of desperation; and, on the 27th of August, he risked a second engagement, on the spot where he had defeated colonel Baillie. Here, however, he was again totally routed; and these successes were followed by a third and a fourth victory over him in the same year; in all of which he displayed uncommon bravery, and had the mortification to see thousands of his best troops cut to pieces.

Although Hyder was still extremely formidable, our victories over him enabled the council to withdraw a part of the troops which had taken the field; and, an expedition was now planned against the Dutch settlements of Negapatam and Trincomalee, the first of which, after a short siege, in which the British sailors displayed their accustomed intrepidity, submitted to our arms; and the latter, owing to the obstinacy of the governor, was taken by storm. The gallant victors, however, gave quarter the moment they entered the fort. They took here about 400 Europeans, with two Indiamen, and a large quantity of stores and ammunition.

Soon after this event, Suffrein, the French admiral, arrived off Coromandel, with 11 ships of the line and several frigates; but, falling in with sir Edward Hughes, near Madras, the English admiral retook six ships that he had captured, which induced the Frenchman to risk an action, in order to recover them. In this, as well as in another which followed soon after, neither party gained any advantage, the ships of sir Edward Hughes and commodore King being reduced almost to a wreck.

These engagements contributed still farther to damp the spirits of Hyder, who had long been expecting relief from the French government; and he soon after experienced another defeat of his own forces before Tellicherry, which place he had blockaded since the commencement of hostilities. But, about the same period, Tippoo Saib contrived to surround 2000 English under colonel Brathwaite, by a body of 15,000 cavalry and 5000 infantry; and yet, however astonishing it may appear, this brave party resisted his repeated attacks for the space of three days, by which time most of the British officers had perished!

During these transactions Hyder received the long expected assistance from France, and immediately captured Cuddalore; but, hearing that the forces under sir Eyre Coote were approaching towards his magazines, at Arnee, he risked another engagement; and though he possessed immense advantages by having his artillery planted on eminences, he was nevertheless again routed by the unparalleled bravery of the English troops.

The next event of importance occurred on the 3d July, 1783, when an engagement took place between the French and English fleets, which terminated greatly to the disadvantage of the former: being, however, joined by some additional ships from Europe, they recaptured Trincomalee, which was not in a condition to stand a siege, and proved a serious loss to the English. Soon after the place had surrendered, sir Edward Hughes arrived off the port with 12 ships of the line, and attacked the French admiral, who had 15 sail; on which occasion much damage was done on both sides, but nothing decisive resulted from the combat.

It was now ascertained, that the French government intended to make a vast effort, in order to recover their influence in India; and many thousands of their regular regiments had already arrived on the coast of Coromandel; but sir Richard Bickerton having also arrived with 5000 troops, the presidency of Bombay was induced to make a powerful diversion towards the kingdom of Mysore, the sovereignty of which had been usurped by Hyder, under the title of Dayva; while he possessed to the northward his favourite kingdom of Canara, a great part of which was denominated Bidnore; but had been changed by him to the name of Hydernagur. Some skirmishing had already taken place in this quarter, in which the British were partially successful, though opposed by six times their number under Tippoo; but, in 1783, the campaign was opened by the grand expedition against the kingdom of Canara, and general Matthews formed the design of carrying the war into the heart of the enemy's country, by the investiture of Onore, a city about 300 miles south of Bombay. This place was soon taken by assault; when a scene of rapine ensued, which, according to the most moderate accounts, could only be equalled by the avaricious oppressions of the Spaniards, in Mexico: a vast sum of money, and a considerable quantity of jewels, were said to have been seized by general Matthews, who was so ardent in the pursuit of plunder, that the army became almost in a state of open mutiny, and many of the principal officers threw up their commissions, and returned in disgust to Bombay.

The same disgraceful scenes were repeated on the capture of the city of Bidnore, which soon followed that of Onore, and in which firstmentioned place, the property seized on by the military, was supposed to amount to 1,200,000l. But the general, after declaring that it was the property of the captors, sent it off, under convoy of his brother, to Bombay, pretending that it had been secured, by the capitulation, to the Mahomedan governor.

The exploits of the English were, however, considerably favoured by the death of Hyder Ally, which occurred towards the end of 1782; but, in the spring of 1783, Tippoo resumed his military operations with great vigour; and, in April, advanced against general Matthews with an army of 150,000 men, with which, having cut off his retreat, he besieged him in Bidnore, where he capitulated, on the conditions, that the English army should be suffered to march out with the honours of war, and return to Bombay; but that the public property should not be molested by them. Tippoo, however, soon broke this treaty, under the pretence that a quantity of the public money had been embezzled; and it was even asserted in some English publications, that, on the surrender of the fort to Tippoo, there was not a single rupee found in it. For this report there indeed seems some foundation, as general Matthews, and about 20 of his principal officers, were seized the next morning, and conducted in chains to Seringapatam, where they were all poisoned with the milk of the cocoa-tree. A short time previous to this event, the general had been deprived of his commission by the supreme council.

During the occurrence of these transactions, the war with the Mahrattas was carried on with considerable success. It was this war which arose from the protection afforded by the British to the assassin Rogonaut Row, and in which Hyder Ally had become a confederate. In 1780, general Goddard had reduced the whole province of Guzerat, stormed the camp of Madajee Scindia, while major Popham captured the important fortress of Gwallior, in the territories of the rajah of Gohud, which had a strong Mahratta garrison, and had always been considered as impregnable.* In the same year, the army of Scindia, consisting of 30,000 men, was defeated by general Carnac; and thus the Mahrattas were induced to conclude a separate peace with the English.

*. See the plate in the Views in Hindostan, and the annexed description.

The pecuniary difficulties of the government, however, were so great, that extraordinary measures were of necessity resorted to. Cheyt Sing, the rajah of Benares, was required to pay 50,000l. as his share of the public burthens, though he had already contributed 240,000l.; and the requisition being continued for three successive years, he exhibited some signs of rebellion, which induced Mr. Hastings to pay him a visit; and, it is asserted, that he not only levied upon him a fine of half a million of money, but put the prince under arrest. His government was then declared vacant, and bestowed on the next heir; by which the revenue derived by the government of Bengal was increased from 240,000l. to 400,000l. per annum. This was one of the principal transactions which caused the important and very singular trial of Mr. Hastings, whose general conduct, after the verdict of the House of Peers, cannot in justice be considered, even by the prejudiced observer of passing events, to have originated in any other motives, than those which were calculated to promote the interests of his country.

At length, on the 19th May, 1783, Tippoo besieged Mangalore, which made the most vigorous resistance under major Campbell, till it was given up by the general pacification, which soon afterwards took place, and confirmed the establishment of the British empire in Bengal.

From this period till the year 1790, India enjoyed a degree of tranquillity to which it had long been unaccustomed; but the restless disposition of Tippoo Saib, with his perpetual and determined hostility towards the Company, which was fostered by the animosity of the French, then induced him to make various infractions on the treaty, by the invasion of the territories of our ally, the nabob. Thus we again saw the flames of war kindled as it were in the heart of our Eastern possessions, and we had no alternative but vigorous resistance. The chief command of the British army now devolved upon lord Cornwallis, seconded by general Abercromby, who was powerfully aided by the warlike Mahrattas; and their united efforts were attended with signal success. The Mahrattas and the Nizam first laid siege to the strong fortresses of Durwar and Copaul, though with little prospect of success, as the enemy appeared to be well supplied with provisions. At the same time Bangalore, the most important place next to Seringapatam, was invested by the British forces under lord Cornwallis; and, while our allies, disheartened by the resistance they had met with, were debating whether they should not convert their sieges into blockades, and thus set their armies at liberty, for more active operations, they received intelligence of the fall of Bangalore. This news, while it elevated the spirit of the besiegers, so far intimidated the garrisons, that they immediately surrendered.

At Bangalore, and in all the conquered forts, the victors found immense supplies of provisions and military stores; and, while lord Cornwallis was endeavouring to form a junction with the Nizam's cavalry, and was occupied in deriving reinforcements from the Carnatic, the allies obtained possession of the whole of the enemy's extensive territories between the Khristna and the Tumbuddra.

These advantages caused so much dismay in Tippoo's army, that he found it advisable to make a precipitate retreat towards Seringapatam, whither he was pursued by the allied forces, with a view to bring him to an action before he could gain his capital. Lord Cornwallis therefore proceeded to Arrakery, a large village about 10 miles from Seringapatam, and encamped there on the 14th of May, 1791, in expectation of being joined by the force under general Abercromby, from whom he was divided by the river Caveri. Here he learned that Tippoo's whole army had encamped between him and Seringapatam, having his right covered by the Caveri, while his left extended along the front of a high mountain, with a deep ravine, the passage of which was defended by batteries; and in which position he had determined to prevent the allies from a nearer approach to his capital. Lord Cornwallis immediately resolved to turn his left flank by a night march, and to cut off the retreat of his main body to the Island of Seringapatam:—this expedition was, however, rendered abortive, owing to several tremendous storms of rain, thunder, and lightning, which threw so many obstacles in the way of the marching army, that they did not come up with the enemy till the middle of the following day; when, after a smart skirmish, in which a party, under colonel Maxwell, drove them from a strong post upon a hill, and captured three pieces of cannon, his lordship found himself under the necessity of retreating to Bangalore, in consequence of his provisions having become alarmingly scarce. Orders were also sent to general Abercromby, to fall back from Periapatam: and it was intended to give the army a few months' refreshment, when an account was received of the approach of two strong Mahratta armies, under the command of Hurry Punt and Purseram Bhow, on whose arrival it was agreed that all the confederate forces should keep the field.

In the mean time Tippoo, with his accustomed duplicity, had made frequent attempts to induce the Peishwa and the Nizam to break off their alliance with the British, and enter into separate treaties with him; but his offers being contemptuously rejected, hostilities recommenced in the autumn, and the strong forts of Rymenghur and Nundy Droog, with very considerable garrisons, were taken by small parties under general Medows and major Gowdie; while Severndroog, a post with 2000 men, and Outradroog, another strong fortification, surrendered to colonel Stuart, with scarcely any loss on his side. These successes were followed by the capture of Darampowry, Pinagra, and Gurrumcandah; all of which were attended with signal instances of bravery on the part of our troops; when, in January, 1792, Tippoo, finding himself reduced to the last extremity, and driven to the very gates of his capital, thought proper to open negotiations for peace; but lord Cornwallis, having learned of a signal instance of treachery on his part, resolved to bring him to a sense of his duplicity, by making a general attack upon his camp. The circumstance was as follows:—Lieutenant Chalmers, with a small body of troops, was besieged at Coimbatoor by Kummer ul Dien Khan; and, after a brave resistance of 28 days, was obliged to capitulate, by which it was agreed, that the garrison should march out with their private property, and be escorted to Paligautcherry; instead of which, after a detention of

13 days at the fort, they were sent prisoners to Seringapatam, by the particular orders of Tippoo.

Hostilities, therefore, recommenced with much vigour; and colonel Ross, commander of the Bombay detachment, accompanied by the armies of the Mahratta chiefs already mentioned, defeated Tippoo's army, which was nearly 10,000 strong, at Semoga, on the 29th December, 1791, when they captured 300 horses, 600 bullocks, and 10 pieces of artillery. The negotiations were then renewed; and lieutenant Chalmers with his party having been sent to the British camp, a preliminary treaty was signed on the 22d of February, 1792, by which one half of the dominions which were in the possession of Tippoo at the commencement of the war was ceded to the allies; and they were remunerated for their expenses by the sum of three crores and 30 lacks of sicca rupees. As a guarantee for the fulfilment of the treaty, Tippoo transmitted to lord Cornwallis his second and third sons, as hostages; and it is but justice to add, that in this instance all his engagements were scrupulously performed. In this war our loss was on the whole so trifling, when compared with that of the enemy, as to form a subject for the astonishment of all military men.

The districts ceded to the allies by this treaty, were found to be productive of the following annual revenuue in pagodas, viz.

| | Pagodas. | | |
|---|---|---|---|
| To the East India Company . . . . . . . . . | 13,16,765 | 5 | 4½ |
| To the Nawaub Assoph Jah Behauder . . . . | 13,16,666 | 6 | 11 |
| To Row Punditt Perdhaun Behauder . . . . . | 13,16,666 | 0 | 0 |
| Total | 39,50,908 | 8 | 9½ |

A few years of peace now succeeded; but this blessing was too evanescent to produce much benefit amongst a people destined as it were by nature to be the sport of conflicting tyrants. In 1798, the ambition and treachery of Tippoo again became manifest; he having, as was afterwards ascertained, planned, as long since as 1792, a project for the complete extirpation of the English from India, as well as for the subversion of the Mahrattas and other Hindoo states, who had long regarded his ambitious career with an eye of jealous suspicion. With this view he had engaged the assistance not only of the French, who have always come forward with alacrity, whenever they could anticipate an opportunity of injuring the vital interests of the British Empire, but of several of the petty sovereigns who were more immediately under his controul. His projects, however, were most happily defeated by the exertions of lord Mornington, now marquis Wellesley, the late governor general:—and the subsequent events of the war, which are too fresh in the memory of Englishmen to need detail, or scarcely to require repetition, conferred additional glory upon the British arms; while the duplicity of the sultaun met with its just reward, by the forfeiture not only of his capital, but of his life!—Thus the whole kingdom of the Mysore was placed at the disposal of our government; while the lesson it afforded to the native princes was such, as effectually to convince them of the futility of prosecuting schemes engendered by ambition, to subvert that power which we have justly attained, by acting on the mere principle of self-defence, while repelling their various acts of agression.

The contest was but of short duration. A vigorous attack upon the enemy's capital was immediately resolved upon; and, on the 4th of May, 1799, the forces under major Beatson effected a breach, and commenced an assault upon Seringapatam, when our troops entered that fortress with a degree of ardour which set all their former efforts at defiance. The garrison made a vigorous resistance, with the sultaun at their head; but they were soon repulsed by our brave army; when the place surrendered to general Harris, and Tippoo's body was shortly afterwards found upon the ramparts, covered with wounds. The whole of his sons, 13 in number, with his harem and all his sirdars thus became prisoners, and we obtained possession of all the strong holds throughout his dominions. It is also worthy of notice, that a correspondence was found in the palace which Tippoo had carried on with the nabob of the Carnatic, the object of which was the subversion of the British influence: in consequence of this discovery, our government seized the whole of that prince's territories, and which the present nabob holds only through our sufferance.*

* The treasure found in Tippoo's palace appears, from various accounts, to have been immense. The value of the jewels was estimated at seven lacks of pagodas, and the merchandize, consisting of rich muslins, shawls, and cloth, at 500 camels' load. The sultaun's throne being too unweildy for conveyance, was broken up. It was a howdar upon a tiger, covered with a sheet of gold, which was found to weigh 40,000 pagodas, while the silver work around it, with the fringe and pearls, were estimated at 10,000 more; the steps were of silver gilt. The canopy was superbly decorated, and of immense value; it was surmounted by a golden bird, with expanded wings: its beak was a large emerald, the wings were lined with diamonds, and the tail was studded with emeralds and other stones, so as to resemble peacocks' feathers. The amount of cash found in the palace was seventeen lacks of pagodas. There

Our preponderance in India thus became firmly established, and it has been still farther consolidated by the glorious events of the last year, which in point of brilliancy are inferior to none in the annals of British valour. The origin of the war with the Mahrattas is well known to all persons connected with India; but, for the information of the general reader, it will merely be sufficient to state, that for many years a strict alliance had subsisted between our government and the Peishwa, who is the nominal and acknowledged head of the Mahratta states, which are also divided amongst several confederated chiefs, descended from Sevagee, the first monarch and founder of the empire; and, as the Peishwa arrived at his dignity not by descent, but from having been prime minister to Sahogee, the third rajah of Sattarah, who delegated to him all the authority of the state, it was natural to expect that a degree of jealousy would exist towards him on the part of the legitimate descendants of the monarch of the empire, though they acknowledged the power conferred upon him by their ancestor. The principal of these chiefs are Scindia, Holkar, the Guikwar, and the rajah of Berar. Scindia's family established themselves in Malwa and Candeish, and afterwards made some conquests amongst the Rajpoots. The family of

were in it, including some of the wives and ladies of the late Hyder and their attendants, *six hundred and fifty females!* The number of men under arms at the assault of Seringapatam, was 2494 Europeans, and 1882 natives—Total 4376. The forlorn hope was led by a sergeant named Graham, belonging to the light company of the Bombay European regiment, who volunteered his services: he ran forward to examine the breach, and mounting it, gave three cheers; on which he returned to his party, and remounted with them with the colours in his hand. On reaching the rampart he placed the colour staff in it, and was at that instant shot through the head!

the Guikwar obtained a great part of Guzerat; while that of Holkar settled themselves in such parts of the province of Malwa as did not belong to Scindia and the Peishwa. These chiefs are independent of each other, and all acknowledge the office of the Peishwa.*

In 1789, lord Cornwallis concluded a treaty with the Peishwa against Tippoo, which gave offence to Scindia and the rajah of Berar, particularly as by the treaty of Seringapatam, in 1792, the Peishwa and the Nizam acquired additional territories. They therefore began to infringe upon the possessions of the Peishwa; and, in 1799, Dowlut Rao Scindia entered the city of Poonah, the Peishwa's capital, with a large army commanded by French officers, and prevented the Peishwa from affording the stipulated assistance to the British, in the war which caused the fall of Seringapatam. Scindia even forced him to carry on a secret correspondence with Tippoo, which being detected, the additional territory intended for the Mahrattas on the conquest of the Mysore, was divided by the marquis of Wellesley's government, between the Nizam and the British. Hence the Mahrattas became our enemies, while we formed an alliance with the Nizam in 1800, and a subsidiary treaty with the Guikwar in 1802, the object of which was to preclude the union of the Mahratta states.

In the mean time the French omitted no means which could tend to restore their influence in the peninsula of India; and,

* We believe the *present* Peishwa obtained his appointment through the influence of Scindia.

having a large force under Monsieur Perron, in the neighbourhood of Agra and Delhi, where they held in the most abject state of subjection Shah Alum, the blind and deposed Mogul emperor, they were prepared to support the interests of Scindia. General Perron succeeded general du Boigne in the command of a strong brigade officered by Frenchmen,* and armed and disciplined according to European tactics. The artillery of this corps was particularly well served and appointed, Scindia having established an extensive foundery instead of purchasing cast fire-arms, as was the previous practice, from British and Dutch settlements. Scindia was the first of the Mahratta chiefs who formed a corps of infantry, their military force being previously confined to cavalry, and these for the greater part mercenaries, whose attachment to any particular leader was dependent on his success, and the prospect of plunder which he held forth. If one of these men lost his horse in battle he was immediately discharged; and this knowledge restrained the natural impetuosity and enterprise of his nature, to the consequent disadvantage of his employer.

By the communications made to the British resident at Hyderabad, by the late Nizam, it appeared that the Berar rajah, who had long been jealous of the growing influence of the British in Hin-

* The force under Perron, however, though French, and their commander influenced by the French government, was not an independent body, but in the pay and under the orders of Scindia:—this force was the object of extreme jealousy to the British government; but, by the treaties it has since imposed on the native princes, they are not at liberty to retain in their service any foreigner whatsoever, without the express permission of the British resident.

dostan, had for a considerable length of time laboured to undermine its interest, and engage the other powers of India in a confederacy against us. With a view to win the Nizam to his purpose he used both threats and promises, and made such communication of his projects, and of his means for their execution, as enabled the governor general to counteract and defeat them.

The dissensions amongst these chiefs had consequently at the period in question attained an alarming height; and, on the 25th of October, 1802, the Peishwa was expelled from his capital; an action having taken place on the same day between the army of Holkar and that of Scindia and the Peishwa, in which the latter combined force was totally defeated. In this dilemma all jealousy towards the British subsided amongst the conquered chiefs, who saw that their only chance of salvation rested on that alliance which they had before rejected. The Peishwa, therefore, conveyed to our government a grant of territory, amounting annually to 25 lacks of rupees, for which he received an auxiliary force of six battalions of sepoys, and a train of artillery: he also expressed his readiness to enter into a strict alliance with our government; and, being conveyed in a British ship to a fort called Sevandroog, in the Cokan, he signed the treaty on the 31st of December, 1802.

In consequence of this treaty the British troops immediately advanced into the Mahratta territories, together with the subsidiary force, and a large body of the Nizam's cavalry; the whole of which arrived at Poonah in the middle of April, 1803, under the command of major general Wellesley, he having received information that

Amrut Rao, who had been placed on the musnud of Poonah by Holkar, meant to plunder and burn the city, having ascertained the impossibility of keeping possession of it. The major general, however, arrived in time to prevent this outrage, and was hailed by the people as their deliverer. The Peishwa was then reinstated, and a proposition was made to Scindia, to admit him a party in the alliance; but the governor general having ascertained that, from the moment of the restoration of the Peishwa, he had been privately attempting to form a confederacy with Holkar, and the rajah of Berar, to usurp the government of Poonah, directions were sent to general Lake, at Cawnpore, to assemble his army on the north-west frontier of the Company's dominions, in order to counteract the intentions of Scindia and the rajah, which had been fully proved to be hostile to the Company, by the intercepting of a correspondence between Scindia and Perron, ordering the latter to prepare for a rupture with the English. It should be observed, that before the commencement of hostilities, every attempt had been made on the part of our government to effect an accommodation; and it was not till colonel Collins (who was sent for this purpose to Scindia's camp) had received the most striking proofs of the duplicity of that chief, that the marquis resolved on hostilities.

These were the primary causes of the war:—its consequences are doubtless still so fresh in the memory of our readers as scarcely to need any repetition. The object of the army under major general Wellesley was to oppose the force of Scindia and the rajah, and thus not only to establish the governments of the Guikwar, of Poonah, and of Hyderabad, but to secure the Company's territory in the Mysore and the Deccan, and to protect the persons of the Nizam and the Peishwa; while that of general Lake was to oppose Perron's forces on the banks of the Jumna, to restore Shah Alum, the deposed Mogul, and to extend the British possessions, by the annexation of Bundelcund, which would give additional security to Benares, while it might check the operations of the Berar rajah.

The plan which had been laid down by the confederates for the prosecution of the war, but which was deranged by the defection of Holkar, was to harass our troops by the rapidity of their movements, to cut off our supplies, to annoy us by ambuscades, and exhaust us by the constant appearance of opposition; but on no account to engage in a general action. The impatience, however, of Scindia, and the confidence he felt in the vast superiority of his numbers, seduced him from this prudent system, in opposition to the advice of the Bhounsla, or rajah of Berar, and involved him in the complete defeat at Assaye, which will be subsequently mentioned. His position, on that occasion, was inconceivably strong by nature, and defended by upwards of 100 pieces of cannon, admirably served:—the army under his command comprised 60,000 cavalry, 11 battalions of infantry, 5000 artillery, and 3000 Arabs, making an effective force of 79,000 men; to this was opposed 1250 European, and about 6000 native troops, namely:

| | |
|---|---|
| Five companies of the 74th regiment, . . . . . . . | 450 men. |
| 78th ditto . . . . . . . | 300 |
| 19th light dragoons, . . . . . | 500 |
| Total Europeans | 1250 |

The 4th, 5th, and 27th regiments of native cavalry, 1st, 8th, 10th, and 12th regiments of native infantry, single battalions.

Perron, in recompense for his services, and for the pay of his brigade, was invested with the sovereignty of a luxuriant and populous tract between the Jumna and the Ganges. The country has since been annexed to the British dominions, but the immense wealth which Perron derived from it has been secured to him.

It would be an act of injustice to the officers entrusted with the important expeditions projected by the British government in India, not to observe, that to their judgment, bravery, and incessant activity, the unexampled success of the campaign is to be in a great measure attributed. The skill and exertions, in short, were such as to astonish even those who are most intimately acquainted with Indian affairs.

The amount of the forces of the confederates in the month of July, 1803, near the Adjuntee Ghaut, was 38,500 cavalry, 10,500 infantry, and 1000 matchlock and rocket men; while those under Perron, in the northern provinces, consisted of about 17,000 infantry, and at least 15,000 cavalry;—total 82,000 men. The army under general Lake consisted of 10,500 men, amongst which there was no more than four or five regiments of Europeans, including infantry, cavalry, and artillery; and about 5500 men who were stationed near Allahabad and Mirzapoor; while the troops under general Wellesley in the Deccan amounted to 16,823, exclusive of a detachment of the 84th regiment at Poonah, and about 1000 sepoys. General Stuart at Moodgul had also a force of 7826 men, with which he afterwards proceeded to Hyderabad.

Thus the enemy had an army nearly double in number to that by which they were opposed, and possessing every local advantage; nevertheless their combined forces were defeated in every direction.

On the 8th of August major general Wellesley commenced his operations by an attack on the fortress of Amednaghur, which capitulated on the 12th, with all the districts dependent on it, and which yielded an annual revenue of 6,34,000 rupees. Scindia had in the mean time entered the territories of the Nizam, who died on the 6th of August; and, being pursued by the major general, a decisive action was fought near Assaye, on the 23d September, in which the enemy was totally routed. The general throughout displayed the greatest bravery, and led in person the 78th regiment to seize the enemy's artillery, in which he had a horse shot under him.

On the 16th of October the city of Boorhanpoor surrendered to colonel Stevenson, as did the important fort of Asseerghur on the 21st; and, on the same day, lieutenant colonel Woodington gained possession of the western face of the fort of Baroach in Guzerat. The whole of the fort was taken by storm on the 29th, on which day general Lake, at a distance of 600 miles, defeated at Coel the forces under Perron. In Cuttack a body of troops under lieutenant colonel Harcourt proved equally successful, driving the Mahrattas from all their strong places in every direction.

On the 4th of September general Lake took by storm the strong fort of Ally Ghur, after a vigorous resistance, in which we sustained considerable loss. The attack was led by lieutenant colonel Monsòn. This place was the grand depot of Perron; and, besides the stores and ordnance, a considerable sum of money was found in it. The most remarkable effect of this capture was that it induced Perron, who, as has been already observed, had long maintained the rank of a sovereign in the country, to resign the service of Scindia, and solicit the protection of the British government, by whom he was received with the greatest respect, and still remains under their protection. It should be added, that he possessed so mean an opinion of the stability of his Indian employer, and of the justice of his own government, that he had long before this event placed all his immense property under the security of the British funds.

The progress of general Lake was now an uninterrupted career of victory: on the 11th he totally defeated the enemy at Delhi; and, after placing the unfortunate Mogul, Shah Alum, under British protection, pursued the fugitive armies towards Agra, where he formed a junction with colonel Vandeleur's detachment, and captured the fort. At Laswarree, on the 1st of November, the British army came up with the enemy, and charged them with their cavalry, in which colonel Vandeleur was killed: and, in the course of that day, a general engagement also took place between the same armies near the village of Mohaulpoor, which, terminating in a splendid victory by our forces, completed the subversion of the hostile confederates, and procured for Great Britain and her allies the most substantial and advantageous treaties.* In this affair the enemy lost about 2000 men, and had an equal number taken prisoners. Our loss was likewise considerable.

* The treaty with the rajah of Berar was signed on the 17th of December, in the camp at Deogoun. It consists of 15 articles, by which it is agreed, that there shall be perpetual peace and friendship between the India Company and the rajah, in consequence of which the latter agrees to cede to the former, in perpetual sovereignty, the province of Cuttack, including the port and district of Balasore; all the territories of which he has collected the revenues jointly with the soubah of the Deccan, and those of which he may have possession, which are to the westward of the river Wurda; the frontier of the rajah towards the territories of the soubah of the Deccan, shall be formed to the west by the river Wurda, from its issue from the Injardy Hills to its junction with the river Godavery. The hills on which the forts of Nernallah and Gawelghur stand, are to remain in possession of the rajah, and all places to the southward of those hills, and to the west of the westward of the river Wurda, to be given up to the British government.—Districts amounting to four lacks of rupees per annum, contiguous to, and to the southward of the abovementioned forts, are to be given up to the rajah.

The rajah also entirely renounces all claims on the territories of the British government, ceded as above, and upon all the territories of the soubah of the Deccan; and engages never to take or retain in his service any Frenchman, or the subjects of any other European or American power, that may be at war with the British government, or any British subject, either European or native, without the consent of the Company. The Company, on their part, agree not to assist any discontented or rebellious relations of the rajah, who, in consequence, renounces all adherence to the confederacy formed by him and Scindia.

The treaty with Scindia was signed on the 30th of December, and consists of 16 articles. By these Scindia cedes to the Company, in perpetual sovereignty, all his forts, territories, and rights in the Douab, and country situated between the Jumna and the Ganges, and all his forts and interests in the countries to the northward of the rajah of Jeypoor and Joodepoor, and of the rajah of Gohud; retaining for himself the countries between Jeypoor and Joodepoor, and to the south of the former. He likewise cedes the fort of Baroach and the territory depending thereon, the fort of Amednaghur and its territory, and all the territories which belonged to him previous to the war, which are situated to the southward of the Adjuntee Hills, including the fort and districts of Jalnapoor, the town and district of Gadnapoor, and all other districts between that range of hills and the river Godavery; and he renounces all claims on the British government and their allies.

Various accounts have been received, which state the revenue that will arise from these treaties to be so considerable as almost to exceed credibility. The most moderate opinion is, that the amount will not be less than 2,000,000 pagodas.

Hence, by their successes against the coalesced native and European forces, the British have acquired an ascendancy in India, of which nothing but an extraordinary want of policy can ever deprive them; while they have taught the natives the salutary lesson, that any future attempt to injure the interests of a nation which may justly be considered as invincible, cannot but terminate in their destruction.

From the various official papers, it appears, that between the 8th of August and the 2d of November, the British army had conquered all the possessions of Scindia in Guzerat, with Boorhanpoor, Cuttack, the Mahratta territories between the Jumna and the Ganges; the cities of Delhi, Agra, and the surrounding country; the fortified town of Amednaghur; the fort of Ally Ghur,* Baroach, Cuttack, Amednaghur,† Powanghur, Champooner, Asseerghur,

* The ordnance found in the fort of Ally Ghur, on the 4th of September, amounted to 33 brass and 60 iron guns, four brass howitzers, two brass mortars, and 182 iron wall pieces. The following is the return of the ordnance captured opposite Delhi on the 11th of September:

Two brass 20-pounders; five ditto 18-pounder carronades; three ditto 16-pounder ditto; three iron 12-pounders (French); 14 brass 6-pounders; one iron 6-pounder; 23 brass 4-pounders; five ditto 3-pounders; four iron 3-pounders; one brass 8-inch mortar; one ditto 8-inch howitzer; four ditto 6-inch howitzers; two ditto $\frac{5}{8}$ ditto; 68 pieces of cannon of different nature: the whole mounted on field-carriages, with limbers and traces complete.—57 tumbrils complete, laden with ammunition; 24 ditto ditto blown up in the field of battle; 61 tumbrils complete, laden with ammunition. The whole of this artillery played on our forces as they advanced; and, except two pieces, it is all found serviceable. Some of them are of the latest French improvement, and have the double property of acting as mortars and howitzers.

† The treasure found in Amednaghur is stated to have been very considerable, and it is supposed much more remained concealed in the fort. The contingent of the Nizam will share prize-money in proportion to the number of his regular troops in the field.

called the key of the Deccan, and Agra, the key of Hindostan. It also gained three general engagements at Delhi, Assaye, and Laswarree, in which were taken the total number of 268 pieces of artillery, 5000 stand of arms, 215 tumbrils, 51 stand of colours, and an immense quantity of stores and ammunition.

Since the general pacification, it appears that hostilities have been renewed by Holkar. General Wellesley had in consequence set off for Poonah on the 17th of May, to take the command of the forces; and colonel Murray, who was stationed in Guzerat, had received orders to join him with a considerable body of troops on Holkar's frontiers. Nothing official has yet transpired; though private accounts, as late as the 27th of May, mention the capture of a strong town of the enemy called Rampoorah, by lieutenant colonel Dunn, and a small body of sepoys. At that period Holkar evidently was not subdued, though it does not require any very intimate knowledge of Indian affairs to anticipate the result of the contest.

The war, however, with Holkar, furnishes a strong illustration of the indecision and fluctuation of Asiatic politics. In the late war he preserved an armed neutrality; in the early progress of it he was negociating with the British government to join it with a subsidiary force of 40,000 men, and this force was for some time held at our disposal, until the rapid and victorious events of that short campaign rendered us superior to the occasion under which his service had been courted. Holkar, profiting by the weakness of Scindia, occupied some of his territory, and instead of a moiety of the revenues of other districts tributary to them both, exacted by military contribution the entire sum. The British government, with equal policy and humanity, declined to advantage itself to the full extent that its victories over Scindia and the Berar rajah might have warranted, obviously with a view to preserve an equalizing, although dependent power in the Mahratta empire; it accordingly guaranteed to Scindia certain of his possessions, granted a subsidiary force of 6000 men, as well to defend as to overawe him, and agreed to the offensive and defensive treaty, under virtue of which it is now engaged in the war which Holkar has commenced against him. Holkar is undoubtedly a man of superior talent and resources; he is brave and enterprising, temperate and decisive; he is, however, greatly deficient in the main sources of Mahratta warfare, money—and his attention is constantly distracted by the jealousy and dissensions of his family. Four of the five great divisions into which the Mahratta empire is separated, viz. the Peishwa, the Guikwar, the rajah of Berar, and Scindia, are in hostility to him; most of the Rajpoots, influenced either by personal hatred or the imposing attitude of this confederacy, have declared against him; the new Nizam is engaged in the war by both these considerations, and the British are urged, by policy and interest, to humble the refractory chief to that state of dependance, to which the other powers of Hindostan are reduced.

THE END.

# GENERAL INDEX

TO

# The Brief History of India.

A.

## GENERAL INDEX.

### B.



### C.

## F.



## G.



## H.

# GENERAL INDEX.



## N.

# GENERAL INDEX.

## O.



## P.



## R.



## S.

## T.



## V.

# GENERAL INDEX.

## W.



## Z.